PSYCHOTHERAPY BY
STRUCTURED LEARNING THEORY

Raymond B. Cattell, Ph.D., D.Sc., London University, is one of the world's leading personality theorists and researchers. As Distinguished Research Professor at the University of Illinois for thirty years he spearheaded a team of internationally acclaimed scholars in their innovative, pioneering research on personality and motivation. This work has been heralded for its creative contributions to personality concepts, psychometric advances, behavioral genetic methods, and clinical, social, and cultural research.

Among Dr. Cattell's many awards are the Darwin Fellowship, the Wenner Gren Prize of the New York Academy of Sciences, distinguished foreign honorary membership in the British Psychological Society, and presidentship of the Society of Multivariate Experimental Psychology. Among his 35 books are the *Handbook of Multivariate Experimental Psychology; Personality and Social Psychology; Prediction of Achievement and Creativity; Abilities: Their Structure, Growth and Action; Meaning and Measurement of Neuroticism and Anxiety;* and *Personality and Learning Theory* (Volumes 1 and 2). His latest work, *Human Motivation and the Dynamic Calculus*, summarizes the motivation research on which the present book rests. He has made over 400 contributions to scientific journals.

Psychotherapy
by
Structured
Learning Theory

Raymond B. Cattell

SPRINGER PUBLISHING COMPANY
New York

Springer Publishing Company, Inc.
536 Broadway
New York, NY 10012

87 88 89 90 91 / 5 4 3 2 1

Library of Congress Cataloging-in-Publication Data

Cattell, Raymond B. (Raymond Bernard), 1905–
  Psychotherapy by structured learning theory.

  Bibliography: p. 165
  Includes index.
  1. Learning—Therapeutic use. 2. Psychotherapy.
3. Learning, Psychology of. 4. Personality. I. Title.
II. Title: Structured learning theory. [DNLM:
1. Learning. 2. Psychotherapy—methods. WM 420
C368p]
RC489.L43C37 1986   616.89'14   85-27790
ISBN 0-8261-5080-2

Printed in the United States of America

Contents

Preface

Practice depends on the advance of the underlying science. The chief advances in measurement-based personality theory in the last generation have been the development of the dynamic calculus and the rise of structured learning theory. But, as far as I know, no proposal has yet been put forward to show where these affect clinical practice. The present work is perhaps a somewhat brash attempt to work out this impact. It is a spearhead of much that will surely follow, as the necessary dependence of diagnosis and therapy on these principles becomes increasingly evident to those now lost in a hundred superficial claims to methods.

Give me extension and motion and I will construct the universe.

— Descartes

Chapter **1**

The Behavioral Equation
for Learning

Since the advances in understanding the human personality made by Freud, Jung, and Adler psychotherapy has progressed little, despite the hubbub of claims. Their claims are myriad, but virtually all are based on quantitatively untested assumptions and on verbal persuasion. Yet the *practice* of psychology must derive from advances in the *science* of psychology, and except for some aspects of behavior therapy, one sees no such attempts at derivation.

The object of this book is to show that a new and positive psycho-therapeutic development is about to take place through the advance of *structured learning theory* — the extension of the science of learning beyond reflexology ("behaviorism"). When patient problems are not due to physiological interference, as in the psychoses, psychotherapy requires of the patient acts of learning and relearning (undoing); it therefore derives, or should derive, directly from the application of the new structured learning theory, developed in personality research.

Structured learning theory is fundamentally different from, and goes much deeper and further than, the classical reflexology of Pavlov, Watson, and Skinner in that it gives due role in learning to what personality research has recognized as *personality and motivation unitary structures*. It does so basically through two important recognitions: (1) that learning is not an atomistic accumulation of conditionings, but a growth of *unitary traits* and recognizable associated processes; and (2) that in any new act of learning *all* the pre-existing personality structures play an active part.

I propose to explain the laws of structured learning as I proceed, though reading elsewhere (e.g., Cattell, 1980, 1981) will help. In the first place, structured learning recognizes five active principles in any learning act:

1. *Coexcitation.* The occurrence of two perceptions at the same time produces a bonding between them, as in one part of the classical conditioning of Pavlov (Skinner's CR I). This occurs, for example, in the babe's association of breastfeeding with the mother.

2. *Means–end.* Any behavior that advances a person toward an instinctual (ergic) goal[1] tends to be learned and repeated. (Skinner's operant conditioning — CR II). For example, by taking a job, a person acquires the means of obtaining food, getting married, etc. Such rewards induce a person toward a stable work life.

3. *Integrative learning.* A new mode of behavior that achieves the goal of two or more existent pieces of behavior will be successfully learned; for example, learning to ask for attention or help instead of trying to evoke it by being helpless, a martyr, or a troublemaker. This involves an extra searching mechanism beyond (2) above.

4. *Sublimation.* Apart from any differences due to means–end learning, the actual *goal* of an erg (at least in the race-preserving ergs, like sex and protective parenting) may itself suffer a substitution, as in sublimation and perversion. For example, satisfactions in art or religion may replace sexual satisfactions without leading, as in (2) above, to a sexual confirmation.

5. *Energy saving.* Of two equally successful courses of action, that course will be preserved (learned) which involves less energy expenditure. This is most obvious in maze learning by rats or humans, wherein superfluous parts are eliminated.

Structured learning theory contends that all changes of behavior or perception arise through one or more of these five principles and that their understanding contributes to correct planning of clinical treatment.

If $a_2 - a_1$ is the magnitude of change in an act j which occurs in response to both a stimulus h and an ambient situation k, then:

$$(a_2 - a_1)_{hjki} = b_{hjk1}T_{1i} + \cdots + b_{hjkp}T_{pi} \tag{1.1}$$

This equation states the learning contribution due to the patient's existing trait levels.

Incidentally, throughout this book we shall stand by the same symbol language: e.g., T for trait, b for behavioral index, a for a measured response in a course of action, and so on. Similarly, h will indicate the focal stimulus to which the person is reacting, by the particular *kind of response* j; k will be the ambient situation, the general condition and background in which the individual i is reacting and which completes the description of the total situation. In learning, j is the kind of thing he is learning and i defines the individual.

The second major innovation in structured learning theory is the proposal that any learning can be represented, as above, in an equation that states (a) how much the patient's existing traits can contribute to the learning, and also in an equation [(1.3) below] that states (b) how the coexcitation, reward, and so forth in the principles above come into action.

Equation (1.1) is familiar to psychologists as the *behavioral equation* for predicting the magnitude of any behavior or behavioral change; it is at present most familiar in educational psychology. It enters, as T_i's, the standard scores of the person, i, on various traits, 1 through p. These p traits are all ability and dynamic traits in the person's profile. Then it weights each trait, according to its relevance in the performance j (in response to stimulus h) by a behavioral index b_{hjkx} peculiar to trait x, to the performance j, the stimulus h, and the general situation k. This is actually a common-sense analysis of all the influences in behaviors, but, with the subscripts, it may look a bit complex.

This behavioral learning equation stops some people at the outset; but it is actually very simple, commonsensical, and practicable for measurement. (Not that we propose to use it with exact numbers for some time; but it is there to remind us of the true complexity of the causes of a particular behavior, when many psychologists speak only of needs,[2] or only of situations, or only of conditioning. This embraces all together.) The dynamic trait unities we here consider established are shown in Table 1.1. Each b value, by its subscripts, is specific to the hjk—the situation and response—and to each trait, T_1 through T_p. That b value, which may vary from $+ 1.0$ to $- 1.0$, states how much the given trait is involved in the learning. For example, if j is solving a mathematics problem, b is probably large for the trait T_g, which is intelligence, and negligible for trait T_e, which is extraversion. The values will be found by correlation of intelligence and extraversion over, say, a sample of 100 people, with a given $(a_2 - a_1)$ where 2 is the postlearning and 1 is the prelearning score.

As an example of the size of the b's, we can take Cattell and Butcher's (1968, p. 187) values for school learning on the standard behavioral equation, which came out as follows:

$$a_{hijk} = .17T_A + .62T_B - .22T_E + .34T_G + .35T_{Q2} \qquad (1.2)$$

This (with lower loading traits included) gives a multiple correlation of .69. Here a is a standard school achievement test measure, T_A is affectia, T_B is intelligence, T_E is dominance, T_G is superego strength, and T_{Q2} is self-sufficiency [on the 16 PF and HSPQ (High School Personality Questionnaire) scales]. These values express (.62) the usual importance of intelligence B, the detraction from learning due to high dominance E, and the help from a strong superego, G—all pretty much as a psychologist would expect, though his estimate of their roles would have to be in the b's.

The actual learning gain $(a_2 - a_1)$ or a_{hijk} on the left can be in any field. It can be the reduction of a symptom, the change of a family attitude, autism, change in a language disorder, a child development sign, a substance abuse—anything with which a clinician or educator has to deal. It is this magnificient generality that justifies our treating it, at the very beginning of our study, as the core enunciation formula of what psychotherapeutic learning is about.

Although the formulae in equations (1.1) and (1.2) above consider the action of the whole personality and the motivation structure of the individual in any learning, the expressions in the ordinary

TABLE 1.1 Ergs and Sems Established by Correlational Research

List of Human Ergs

Goal Title	Emotion	Status of Evidence
Food-seeking	Hunger	Replicated factor; measurement battery exists
Mating	Sex	Replicated factor; measurement battery exists
Gregariousness	Loneliness	Replicated factor; measurement battery exists
Parental	Pity	Replicated factor; measurement battery exists
Exploration	Curiosity	Replicated factor; measurement battery exists
Escape to security	Fear	Replicated factor; measurement battery exists
Self-assertion	Pride	Replicated factor; measurement battery exists
Narcistic sex	Sensuousness	Replicated factor; measurement battery exists
Pugnacity	Anger	Replicated factor; measurement battery exists
Acquisitiveness	Greed	Replicated factor; measurement battery exists
Appeal	Despair	Factor, once replicated; battery exists
Rest-seeking	Sleepiness	Factor, but of uncertain independence
Constructiveness	Creativity	Factor, but of uncertain independence
Self-abasement	Humility	Factor, but of uncertain independence
Disgust	Disgust	Factor absent for lack of markers
Laughter	Amusement	Factor absent for lack of markers

List of Human Sentiments

Symbol Title	Symbol Title
S_1 *Profession* (1)	S_{15} *Theoretical-logical.* Thinking, precision (2) (8) (10)
S_2 *Parental family, home* (1)	S_{16} *Philosophical-historical.* Language, civics, sociocultural, esthetic rather than economic (2) (3) (6) (7)
S_3 *Wife, sweetheart* (1)	
S_4 *The self-sentiment* (1). Physical and psychological self	
S_5 *Superego* (1)	S_{17} Patriotic-political (1) (7)
S_6 *Religion.* This has emphasis on doctrine and practice, on high social and low esthetic values (1) (4) (7) (8)	S_{18} *Sedentary-social games.* Diversion, play, club and pub sociability; cards (2) (10)
S_7 *Sports and fitness.* Games, physical activity, hunting, military activity (1) (2) (3)	S_{19} *Travel-geography.* Possibly Guildford's autism here
S_8 *Mechanical interests* (1) (2) (5)	S_{20} *Education-school attachment*
S_9 *Scientific interests.* High theoretical, low political; math. (2) (3) (4) (5) (6) (7) (9)	S_{21} *Physical-home-decoration-furnishing*
	S_{22} *Household-cooking*
	S_{23} *News-communication.* Newspaper,

(*continued*)

TABLE 1.1 (*Continued*)

S_{10} *Business-economic.* Money administrative (2) (3) (4) (5)	radio, TV
S_{11} *Clerical interests* (2) (4)	S_{24} Clothes, self-adornment
S_{12} *Esthetic expressions* (2) (10)	S_{25} Animal pets
S_{13} *Esthetic-literary appreciation.* Drama	S_{26} Alcohol
S_{14} *Outdoor-manual.* Rural, nature-loving, gardening, averse to business and "cerebration" (2) (5) (6)	S_{27} Hobbies not already specified

[a]Numbers in parentheses are references, as follows. (1) Cattell et al. (4 studies); (2) Guildford et al. (1954); (3) Thurstone (1935); (4) Gundlach and Gerum (1931); (5) Torr (1953); (6) Carter, Pyles, Bretnall (1935); (7) Ferguson, Humphreys, Strong (1941); (8) Lurie (1937); (9) Strong (1949); (10) Thorndike (1935). See also (11) Cottie (1950); (12) Hammond (1945); (13) Crissy and Daniel (1939); (14) Vernon (1950); (15) Miller (1968).

The references for these researches are in Cattell (1979) and Cattell and Child (1975).

Source: From *Personality and Learning Theory* Vol. 1, (pp 143, 145) by R. B. Cattell. New York: Springer Publishing Company, 1979. © 1979 Springer Publishing Co.

behavioral equation are incomplete. They do not refer to the second part of the determiners — the reward and so forth in the detailed role of the above five principles, working in the various learning equations which follow. We may pause for a moment to illustrate this working of principles, in addition to the traits in (1.2), as follows:

$$(a_2 - a_1)_{hijk} = b_{hjk1}T_{1i} + \cdots + b_{hjkp}T_{pi} + b_{hjke}C_i$$
$$+ b_{hjkm}ME_i + b_{hjk1}I_i + b_{hjks}S_i + b_{hjke}E_i \qquad (1.3)$$

Here the T's are all kinds of trait scores (abilities, personality traits, etc.) and the C's, ME's, S's, and so forth are the contributions from each of the five principles.

Here the b's are simply the discovered weights for ability, personality, and dynamic traits — the behavioral indices on the given learning.

It must be admitted that (1.3) is a crudely simplified, descriptive statement, for we must advance to incorporate the *interaction* of the traits with the principles. This is represented in one term in equation (1.3), namely, $b_{hjkm}ME_i$. This states the reward gain in the person's dynamic traits: the ergs, E. It is more fully expressed in equation (1.4), where $(E_1 - E_2)$ is the reduction of tension (i.e., the reward) on the E's, and M is the extent to which the sems cause these ergs to be involved in the given learning.

$$(a_2 - a_1)_{hijk} = \sum^{x=g} b_x T_{xi} + \sum^{y=p} b_y M_{yi}(E_{1y} - E_{2y}) + b_c C_i E_i + b_s S_i E_i$$
$$+ b_i I_i E_i + b_{su} S_{ui} E_i \qquad (1.4)$$

(The *hjk* subscript is omitted from all the *b*'s.)

This puts all personality trait effects in the first term and all reward effects in the second. The effects from co-excitation, energy saving, integrated learning, and sublimation follow in the terms C, S, I, and S_u. The subscript i says that these are the magnitudes of the experience for the given individual, i. The E's enter these terms because the sublimation, energy saving, etc. act upon given strengths of E's. Thus equation (1.4) is simply a more detailed statement of what is expressed in general terms in equation (1.3).

A learning that involves a sublimation, S, experience [making a loss or gain in $(a_2 - a_1)$] operates also on E, transforming it to an E', which now has an effect like an E but is different in its id origin. The *b*'s in (1.1) above are of course to be found by factor analysis, or by correlating the measures of the T's, etc., with a gain $(a_2 - a_1)_{hjki}$.

Although, as already stated, clinical practice has not yet advanced to the level of determining b values for needed predictions, we can rightly *estimate* some weights for specific traits in some behaviors. Thus, from the literature on suicide, one can make the following guesses about weights on the 16 PF primary personality factors:

$$\text{Suicide likelihood} = -.2A - .5C - .2E - .6F$$
$$+ .4G + .4O + .4Q_4 \qquad (1.5)$$

This particular equation is actually derived from the evaluation by Karson and O'Dell (1976). For another clinically important behavior, recovery from alcoholism, which has several forms, we can only very tentatively write:

$$\text{Recovery} = .4C + .1E + .4F + .5G + .4O - .5Q_4 \qquad (1.6)$$

Although the formulae in (1.1) and (1.2) above consider the action of *the whole personality and motivation structure* of the individual in any learning, they are incomplete in not giving the second contributor the detailed role of the five principles listed earlier. In life situations the contribution of these "principles" may not be as large as the trait contribution. As the .69 prediction of school achievement in equation (1.2) evidences, there is not much left for prediction from circumstances of reward, etc. We recognize, however, that the advance of one child may receive more applause from his family than that of another. Clearly the full structured learning equation *should* contain terms for these determiners, which, as far as reward and dynamic traits go (D's, including E's and M's), will generally make the second part of the equation appear as in equation (1.7). That is, it will weight, by b's, the rewards on all ergs and sems relevant to the task, as in equation (1.7).

$$\text{Gain from means–end reward} = b_{r1}(D_{11} - D_{12})$$
$$+ \cdots b_{rp}(D_{p1} - D_{p2}) \qquad (1.7)$$

for p dynamic traits on learning of behavior r.

This says that, between the beginning and the end of the learning run, the dynamic trait, e.g. erg, D, falls in its tension level from D_{11} to D_{12}, and this reduction is the strength of the reward on D_1. Similar reductions take place on other dynamic traits, up through the pth trait. Since we have no certainty that a reduction in tension on, say, sex erg, has the same power in committing to memory as a corresponding reduction on fear, we have to put b weights in (1.7) to meet the facts of degree of engramming obtained.

There would be "effect" equations like (1.7) above added to equations (1.1) and (1.2) for each of the remaining four principles. Even this is not quite the end of the complications, as will be seen later; but it is a first "bird's-eye view" of what goes on in learning. We should note that, among the possible complications in the total learning gain, are a split into a contribution in *committing to memory* (engramming strength) and in *recall*, which could be different — the latter depending on the dynamic forces brought to bear in bringing an engram to expression. However, these complexities can at present be set aside in our main realization that the total personality, along with the learning principles in equation (1.3), enters into any act of learning or relearning. This is the first proposition of structured learning theory. We know the b weights so far for only a few learnings — for example, various school subjects, recovery from neurosis and delinquency — but we have the measurement instruments in the 16 PF, Clinical Analysis Questionnaire (CAQ), Motivational Analysis Test (MAT), and so forth for determining all that is of interest to the therapist in the traits that are at work and weighted. The determination of b's — the behavioral indices describing the effect of various situations — is a matter for current psychotherapeutic basic research.

NOTES

[1]The term *erg* corresponds to what used to be called an *instinct*. Nowadays, as the result of dynamic variable experiments, it has the more precise operational meaning of being a demonstrable independent *factor* in a factor analysis of motivation, dynamic attitude measures. Among the ergs so far discovered (and measured in the Motivation Analysis Test, MAT) are sex, self-assertion, narcism, gregariousness, and fear (escape).

Evidently the id itself is not yet caught and measurable. It undoubtedly exists as a *fund* of these unconscious ergic (rhymes with *allergic*) demands, blind yet purposive, controlled in its expression by the ego, the super ego, and all the sentiments (sems). The question of whether it can be revealed as a *general dynamic* demand factor can only be answered in individual difference terms, when we use objective test measures of interest strength that are real and not half ipsative. Meanwhile, we must accept the id as the ergic basis of all behavior, conscious and unconscious, probably to be found as a third- or fourth-order factor in such motivation measures. (It is hypothesized also to exist in the *style* motivation components, as CX, loading autism, fantasy, distortion of reasoning, id projection, and simple "I want" statements. See p. 72.)

[2]*Needs* is replaced here by *ergs*, aided by *sems* (short for *sentiments*). The evidence for the validity of ergs and sems as distinct entities rests on several factor analyses like that in Table 1.1, on two forms for each of the attitudes measured.

The meanings of these factored ergs and sems here are discussed in the text. Obviously the clinician needs to develop precise concepts of each temperament and dynamic trait, as developed in more detail in the test Handbooks, in Karson and O'Dell (1976), in Krug (1971), and in Heather Cattell's clinical volume, *Diagnosis in Clinical Practice* (1986). The meanings, however, should become clear in the rest of this book.

Chapter **2**

What Is the
Aim of Therapy?

The aims of therapy have been variously stated. People come with all kinds of needs, such as reduction of a phobic system, reduction of a trait such as anxiety, the improvement of an interpersonal relationship, and so on. We shall deliberately omit here the cure of a psychosis, since the most prevalent psychoses — schizophrenia and manic-depressive disorder — rest on a hereditary physioneural defect requiring chemotherapy, with psychotherapy useful only as an aid.

Looked at from the standpoint of the behavioral equation, therapy clearly reduces to changing behavior, which by the structured learning model of equations (1.1), (1.2), and (1.3) can be done in *only two ways*: changing the level of a trait — a T in equation (1.1); or changing the weight of a behavioral index — a b in the learning in equation (1.3). Only by either or both of these can the size of the act a be changed, that is, a significant $(a_2 - a_1)$ score be produced.

This, incidentally, is a new view of what learning means. The animal laboratory learning investigators measured learning, up to the present time, simply as $(a_2 - a_1)$ and plotted learning curves accordingly. But the structured learning theorist realizes that the learning can only be fully described by discovering and listing the changes in the T levels *and* in the b levels, which greatly enriches the meaning of the given learning.

Indeed, he recognizes that it is possible for learning to occur with *no* change in the level of the performance $(a_2 - a_1)$! The person then simply uses a new combination of T scores, from a different *b* combination, to produce the same gross effect. As Fleishman (1967) showed, a person may achieve the same level of motor performance in a second trial by using more of the trait of motor skill and less of intelligence than he did in a first trial. The *b*'s have altered, but the traits — and the performance — can remain at the same level! This has been checked by Hendricks (1971) in terms of personality traits in learning. The case of no change in the performance itself would be somewhat unusual, but it suffices to remind us of what every mathematician looking at the equations knows can happen, and which happens for reasons that an observant psychologist can recognize. For example, the first time a person applies for a job he is likely to depend on a certain suppressed boldness (*H* factor) and good use of intelligence, whereas the second time the call on boldness may be greater and the call on verbal ability may be less.

Invariance, i.e., lack of change of actual performance under learning, is a special case, illustrating how flexibly the behaviorial equation can realistically represent behavior. But the analysis reminds us that in the broad context of therapy the aims of the therapist can always be two: to bring *different* traits and resources to bear in certain situations (i.e., to change the *b*'s) and to increase or decrease certain traits, *T*'s, such as anxiety or dominance. We know that although traits like dominance (*E* factor) and superego strength (*G* factor), taken as 16 PF measures, are normally reasonably stable (though not as stable as, say, the I.Q. trait) and are liable to moderate changes through life events. For example, as Barton and Cattell (1972a,b, 1975) have shown, dominance (*E* factor) falls as a result of a prolonged illness, superego strength (*G* factor) increases with years of marriage, and surgency (*F* factor) declines with assumption of heavy responsibilities. When the therapist perceives, from his diagnostic measures (e.g., the *CAQ* or the 16 PF), which factors need to be increased or decreased [according to their role in the symptom in equation (1.1)], he has to find a way to induce those trait changes (along with the changes in the *b*'s). The presently checked primary personality source traits (see Table 3.3 in the next chapter) are as listed in Tables 2.1 and 2.2.

It will rightly be objected that equation (1.1) refers to *change* in a *single* performance, and that the actual performance formula may need to be somewhat different, as in the standard extended behavioral equation, repeated with extension of meaning from equation (1.3), thus

$$a_{hijk} = b_{hjk1} T_{1i} + b_{hjk2} T_{2i} + \cdots + b_{hjkp} T_{pi} \qquad (2.1)$$

where a_{hijk} may be a broad and complex "performance" like "success during a year in college," "making a success of marriage," or "abstaining from substance abuse," measured over a period.

In this equation, incidentally, the p traits always include three modalities: (1) abilities and cognitive traits, (2) general personality traits such as ego and superego strength, and (3) dynamic traits, such as sentiment to home, the erg (need) for security, and so on. If, where a_{hjk} is a very specific behavior, j, in a specific situation, hk, one alters the involvement of these traits—the b's—in a given behavior (e.g., avoiding company, having a phobia for cats), one alters only the *level* of that particular behavior (e.g., avoiding company, having a phobia for cats). Altering b's is possible without changing the total personality: this may suffice for some cases, as it does in much behavior therapy. But more frequently a major therapeutic job calls for change in a personality trait, for example, ego strength (C), dominance (E), or shyness $(H-)$, as well as in the b's.

Every patient comes with a problem, and the first task in the interviews that follow testing is to ascertain what it is. In the first place, we must recognize the difference between an *external world* problem [see the first part of the Adjustment Process Analysis (APA) Chart, Figure 9.1)] such as a frustrating situation or an inappropriate expression, and an *internal problem* (see the second part of the APA) generating anxiety, or a compulsion, or an identity problem, or a drug addiction, or some other neurotic symptom.

The aim of therapy in the first case is to help the patient find some acceptable outlet for the frustrated or inappropriately expressed need. As Adler said years ago, the life problems fall into three areas: sex, subsistence, and society, i.e., marriage, job, and social relations. The new outlet must be found in behavior that can be free

TABLE 2.1 List of Normal Personality Source Traits

Source-trait symbol	Low-score description	High-score description	Number of items in each form in 16 PF (HSPQ and CPQ essentially similar)		
			AB	CD	EF
A	SIZIA Reserved, detached, critical, aloof, stiff	AFFECTIA Outgoing, warmhearted, easygoing, participating	10	6	8
B	LOW INTELLIGENCE Dull	HIGH INTELLIGENCE Bright	13	8	8
C	LOWER EGO STRENGTH At mercy of feelings, emotionally less stable, easily upset, changeable	HIGHER EGO STRENGTH Emotionally stable, mature, faces reality, calm	13	6	8
E	SUBMISSIVENESS Humble, mild, easily led, docile, accommodating	DOMINANCE Assertive, aggressive, competitive, stubborn	13	6	8
F	DESURGENCY Sober, taciturn, serious	SURGENCY Happy-go-lucky, gay, enthusiastic	13	6	8
G	WEAKER SUPEREGO STRENGTH Expedient, disregards rules	STRONGER SUPEREGO STRENGTH Conscientious, persistent, moralistic, staid	10	6	8
H	THRECTIA Shy, timid, threat-sensitive	PARMIA Venturesome, uninhibited, socially bold	13	6	8

	Low Pole	High Pole			
I	HARRIA — Tough-minded, self-reliant, realistic	PREMSIA — Tender-minded, sensitive, clinging, overprotected	10	6	8
L	ALAXIA — Trusting, accepting conditions	PROTENSION — Suspicious, hard to fool	10	6	8
M	PRAXERNIA — Concerned with practical and concrete details. Practical minded.	AUTIA — Interested only in general ideas, imaginative, bohemian in lifestyle			
N	ARTLESSNESS — Forthright, unpretentious, genuine, but socially clumsy	SHREWDNESS — Astute, polished, socially aware	10	6	8
O	UNTROUBLED ADEQUACY — Self-assured, placid, secure, complacent, serene	GUILT PRONENESS — Apprehensive, self-reproaching, insecure, worrying, troubled	13	6	8
Q_1	CONSERVATISM OF TEMPERAMENT — Conservative, respecting traditional ideas	RADICALISM — Experimenting, liberal, free-thinking	10	6	8
Q_2	GROUP ADHERENCE — Group-dependent, a "joiner" and sound follower	SELF-SUFFICIENCY — Self-sufficient, resourceful, prefers own decisions	10	6	8
Q_3	LOW SELF-SENTIMENT INTEGRATION — Undisciplined self-conflict, lax, follows own urges, careless of social rules, low self-esteem	HIGH STRENGTH OF SELF-SENTIMENT — Controlled, exacting will power, socially precise, compulsive, following self-image, high esteem	10		8
Q_4	LOW ERGIC TENSION — Relaxed, tranquil, torpid, unfrustrated, composed	HIGH ERGIC TENSION — Tense, frustrated, driven, overwrought	13	6	8

TABLE 2.2 List of Abnormal Personality Source Traits

Source-trait symbol	Low-score description (1–3)	High-score description (8–10)
D_1	LOW HYPOCHONDRIASIS Is happy, mind works well, does not find ill health frightening	HIGH HYPOCHONDRIASIS Shows overconcern with bodily functions, health, or disabilities
D_2	ZESTFULNESS Is contented about life and surroundings, has no death wishes	SUICIDAL DISGUST Is disgusted with life, harbors thoughts or acts of self-destruction
D_3	LOW BROODING DISCONTENT Avoids dangerous and adventurous undertakings, has little need for excitement	HIGH BROODING DISCONTENT Seeks excitement, is restless, takes risks, tries new things
D_4	LOW ANXIOUS DEPRESSION Is calm in emergency, confident about surroundings, poised	HIGH ANXIOUS DEPRESSION Has disturbing dreams, is clumsy in handling things, tense, easily upset
D_5	HIGH-ENERGY EUPHORIA Shows enthusiasm for work, is energetic, sleeps soundly	LOW ENERGY, FATIGUED DEPRESSION Has feelings of weariness, worries, lacks energy to cope
D_6	LOW GUILT AND RESENTMENT Is not troubled by guilt feelings, can sleep no matter what is left undone	HIGH GUILT AND RESENTMENT Has feelings of guilt, blames self for everything that goes wrong, is critical of self

D_7

LOW BORED DEPRESSION
Is relaxed, considerate, cheerful with people

HIGH BORED MISANTHROPIC DEPRESSION
Avoids contact and involvement with people, seeks isolation, shows discomfort with people

PA

LOW PARANOIA
Is trusting, not bothered by jealousy or envy

HIGH PARANOIA
Believes he is being persecuted, poisoned, controlled, spied on, mistreated

PP

LOW PSYCHOPATHIC DEVIATION
Avoids engagement in illegal acts or breaking rules, sensitive

HIGH PSYCHOPATHIC DEVIATION
Has complacent attitude toward own or other's antisocial behavior, is not hurt by criticism, likes crowds

SC

LOW SCHIZOPHRENIA
Makes realistic appraisals of self and others, shows emotional harmony and absence of regressive traits

HIGH SCHIZOPHRENIA
Hears voices or sounds without apparent source outside self, retreats from reality, has uncontrolled and sudden impulses

AS

LOW PSYCHASTHENIA
Is not bothered by unwelcome thoughts and ideas or compulsive habits

HIGH PSYCHASTHENIA
Suffers insistent, repetitive ideas and impulses to perform certain acts

PS

LOW GENERAL PSYCHOSIS
Considers self good, dependable, and smart as most others

HIGH GENERAL PSYCHOSIS
Has feelings of inferiority and unworthiness, timid, loses head easily

of undesirable new problems — and present a permanently reward-ing, stable way of behaving. To scout the possibilities with the patient, the therapist needs not only measures of the ability and per-sonality traits (as provided by the 16 PF, HSPQ, CAQ, or Objec-tive–Analytic (O–A) batteries) but also measures of the relative level of the patient's basic needs (provided by the MAT (or, with children, the SMAT — school motivation analysis test). The making of these measures we shall discuss soon.

In the case of the internal problems, one has to unravel a history of "progress" to definable positions along the APA Chart. This in-volves uncovering early emotional miseducation, trauma, frustra-tions, and unconstructive reactions to frustrations that have estab-lished maladjustive habits of thinking and acting. The behavior therapist may simply think in terms of reconditioning, but the general therapist looks at broad fields of adjustment in sex, sub-sistence, and society, that is, in marriage, job, and social relations.

In the case of the internal problems one has to unravel a history of past "progress" along the APA Chart. This involves uncovering early emotional mis-education, trauma, frustrations, and uncon-structive reactions to frustrations that have established maladjustive habits of thinking and acting. The behavior therapist may seek to effect only the final outcome of this historical train by means of systematic reward and punishment (deprivation), leaving the older tangle untouched. But to the psychoanalyst it seems necessary to work back through that tangle and attempt to establish more healthy, less past-bound responses.

Structured learning therapy differs from both of these meth-ods, but in different ways. In the first place, the therapist brings to bear diagnostically the instruments of functional psychological testing (Cattell and Johnson, 1986). During therapy he monitors the changes in traits, on the tests just mentioned. But he can only guess at the success in bringing about changes in b's because (1) research has not established the normal b values in a healthy sample of the population for an important variety of behaviors, and (2) without this group (R-technique information on b's), he can only make b comparisons *within the patient* by the practice called P-technique (Birkett and Cattell, 1978). This deluxe method, until further advanced, demands an amount of time and testing (at least 100 hours per patient) impracticable for most practitioners and patients. There is also the problem that the *b*'s usually need to be therapeutically changed for several behaviors, not just one.

Thus, although we have reduced the goals of therapy to a clear and adequate model, we cannot fully apply it until clinicians complete more research on values in the behavioral equations. Nevertheless, we can claim to have reduced the ultimate goals of all forms of therapy to clear essentials, around which the aims of diagnosis and therapy can be intelligently organized and appraised.

Chapter 3

Testing Traits and Trait Changes

Although we are eager to push on to the principles of structural therapeutic action, it would be a mistake to do so in a vacuum, without an up-to-date understanding of the actual trait structures involved.

Many psychologists presently seem content to assess the patient's personality in the therapeutic sessions, without first availing themselves of the new resources of psychometry. They may even be rather vague about what common traits to look for, or be content with oversimplified designations — like "introvert or extravert," "given to external versus internal control," or other arbitrary dichotomies.

The results of fifty years of broadly based factor analytic study show that human nature is much more complex than what can be measured on, say, the three factors of Eysenck, or the five factors of the MMPI (which covers only five-factor analytically independent dimensions, despite all its scales). The number of general normal personality factors is shown by factor analysis to be about 23, and, adding abnormal behavior, we have found an additional 12 factors covered now in the CAQ, leaving us with a rather formidable list of 35 trait concepts.

The largest 17 or 18 of the normal factors are now covered by the age-adjusted family progression of questionnaires, found in the 16 PF, the HSPQ, the CPQ (Child Personality Questionnaire), the ESPQ (Early School Personality Questionnaire — ages 6 to 8), and so on. The 12 abnormal dimensions are added to the 16 of the PF to produce the comprehensive 28 factors of the CAQ.

It is as impossible to describe in detail here all the primary ability, temperament, and dynamic factors presently known as it would be to describe the properties of all the elements in a book on applied chemistry. For a recent full account, the reader is referred to *Functional Psychological Testing* by Cattell, Johnson, et al. (Brunner Mazel, New York, 1986). However, the following lists will give the reader an overview of the concepts dealt with in this book [excepting the primary abilities set out in Cattell & Hakstian (1974)]. The bibliography of supporting, factor analytic researches is given in *Personality and Mood by Questionnaire* (Cattell, 1973b) and elsewhere, including analysis of criticisms.

There are nine established second-order factors back of these twenty-eight primaries, which, with their validities, are shown in Table 3.1. These factors and validity coefficients are derivable from 16 PF and CAQ primary scores.

Dynamic traits from the list on p. 5, which have been cut down to the 10 most important for clinical practice, are defined as shown in Table 3.2, taken from the *MAT Handbook*.

The evidence for their validity rests on several confirmatory factor

TABLE 3.1 Direct Concept Validities of the Second-Order Factors

Factor	Validity coefficient
Extraversion	.85
Anxiety	.83
Tough Poise	.69
Independence	.76
Superego	.74
Socialization	.81
Depression	.95
Psychosis	.83
Neuroticism	.71

Note: Based on data from 1,915 normal and clinically diagnosed adults. See Krug & Laughlin (1976).

analyses like those in Table 3.2, based on four *objective* devices for each of the attitudes measured.

The meaning of *ergs* and *sems* (sentiments) has been discussed earlier. Obviously the clinician needs to develop precise concepts of each temperament and dynamic trait, as developed in more detail in the *MAT Handbooks*, in Karson & O'Dell (1976), in Krug (1977b), and in Heather Cattell's clinical volume, *Diagnosis in Clinical Practice* (1986). The meanings, however, should become clear in the rest of this book.

For the correlational factor structure of the 16 PF and CAQ together, see Table 3.3.

If one is suspicious of the questionnaire as a method, he has available the O–A battery of performance tests of personality, so far covering the 10 largest factors found in that area.

All of the factors have predictive value clinically. Figures 3.1, 3.2, and 3.3 show, for example, the mean profiles of anxiety neurotics, criminals, and homosexuals.

Factor *A*, labeled "affectia-vs.-sizia," separates emotional responsiveness and social adaptability from rigidity and withdrawal. As *A* indicates, it is the first *largest* factor in both ratings and questionnaires, and corresponds to the psychiatric distinction (Bleuler, 1933; Kretschmer, 1925) of cyclothymes and schizothymes, being apparently temperamental. Factor *B* in the 16 PF, HSPQ, CPQ, etc., is the next largest factor, intelligence. Factor *C*, the Freudian ego strength, is a very important factor, being at a low score in all pathological cases. Factor *E* is dominance; *F* is surgency-vs.-desurgency; *G* is supergo — and so on to Q_4, which represents the amount of unexpressed libido (ergic tension).

In the morbidity factors included in the CAQ, we find 7 depression factors, of varying nature and causes, which should give guidance for various kinds of medication. We also find such factors measured on the MMPI as schizophrenia, hysteria, paranoia, and psychopathic tendency, but there only as "differentiator" items on types. The nature of the 28 factors in the CAQ must be pursued, in more detail, in its Handbook. Their reality rests on numerous factor analytic re-checks on personality structure, as shown in Table 3.3.

Beyond the questionnaires lie the objective performance tests of

TABLE 3.2 Evidence for the Dynamic Factor Structure of the MAT

ATTITUDES	FACTORS (Pattern)										
I want:	Fear	Mating	Assertiveness	Narcism	Pugnacity	Self-sentiment	Superego	Career	Sweetheart	Home-parental	Residual
1. Protection from A-Bomb	55	-18	-32	-06	45	00	-17	10	-13	16	-26
2. To avoid disease, injury	84	-01	-21	16	-20	-16	12	20	04	-12	-15
3. To fall in love	04	68	11	09	10	09	11	-28	-18	07	06
4. To satisfy sexual needs	-16	60	12	08	-14	-06	-10	08	03	-38	-01
5. To dress smartly	-18	01	67	25	-21	-23	03	-29	-21	29	-06
6. To increase salary, status	24	17	47	16	-28	16	02	32	-16	-30	-06
7. To enjoy delicacies	62	-20	16	58	10	14	-00	03	11	-05	19
8. To rest, have easy time	-13	-01	47	24	31	43	-07	-20	17	-35	38
9. To destroy our enemies	-07	-20	17	05	80	-06	14	04	07	-07	-00
10. To see violent movies	02	25	-23	55	38	-22	-05	-00	02	-21	-09
11. To control impulses	32	-07	-05	-12	14	42	31	-29	09	-06	-59
12. Never to damage self-respect	-10	-11	-08	17	-13	90	-06	16	11	06	04

13. To maintain reputation	-22	-34	03	42	-29	58	26	-04	-29	01	-12
14. Never to be insane	05	23	06	09	14	84	30	06	-04	15	-15
15. A normal sexual adjustment	17	55	02	-07	22	47	-04	28	25	19	10
16. To know myself better	44	13	01	-04	-09	43	10	-18	06	09	18
17. To look after family	23	-19	-08	-02	-00	16	01	-08	-04	36	71
18. To be proficient in career	37	10	69	11	22	45	-12	19	-04	17	-07
19. To satisfy sense of duty	06	-21	19	-15	-15	-08	61	25	23	-10	-41
20. To end all vice	-07	17	-68	-18	-00	34	55	17	-09	-03	19
21. To be unselfish	-04	06	19	-01	10	02	73	-03	10	10	12
22. To avoid impropriety	05	19	-27	09	-17	-04	82	-10	-11	23	-18
23. To learn my job well	04	02	25	17	00	08	04	79	05	-03	07
24. To stick with my job	13	05	-15	-61	-11	-11	35	58	-03	-16	07
25. To spend time with sweetheart	-05	-11	-11	11	00	-01	-02	-07	83	13	06
26. To bring gifts to sweetheart	03	12	10	-06	01	-00	01	01	83	13	-09
27. My parents to be proud of me	-11	09	28	-01	-03	26	01	04	08	80	-06
28. To depend on my parents	10	-00	09	-20	-23	-00	-05	-05	-00	87	09

Source: From Handbook for the Motivation Analysis Test "MAT" (p. 18) by R. B. Cattell, J. L. Horn, A. B. Sweney, and J. A. Radcliffe. Champaign, IL, 1959. © 1959 Institute for Personality and Ability Testing. Reprinted by permission.

TABLE 3.3 Evidence for Loading Patterns on Four Researches on 28 Personality Primaries, Normal, and Abnormal (16 PF and CAQ)

	A				B				C				E				F				G		
	1	2	3	4	1	2	3	4	1	2	3	4	1	2	3	4	1	2	3	4	1	2	3	4
A_1	70	65	48	51																				
A_2	58	60	70	49																				
B_1					49	65	76	84																
B_2					69	66	59	84								32								
C_1									33		54	36												
C_2									51	55	37													
E_1									38				68	38	49	88								
E_2													65	63	26	71								
F_1																	46	74	64	40				
F_2																	43	44	37	79				
G_1																				−31	72	55	55	42
G_2																					62	73	67	68
H_1													31							40				
H_2																				36				
I_1																								
I_2																								
L_1																								
L_2																								
M_1																	40							
M_2																								
N_1									−37															
N_2																								
O_1									33															
O_2																								
Q_{11}																								
Q_{12}							−31													−30			−30	

26

	Study 1	Study 2	Study 3	Study 4
Q_{21}				
Q_{22}				
Q_{31}			52	36
Q_{32}				
Q_{41}				
Q_{42}				
D_{11}	35			
D_{12}	94			
D_{21}				
D_{22}				
D_{31}				
D_{32}			39	
D_{41}				
D_{42}		-38		
D_{51}				
D_{52}			-32	
D_{61}				
D_{62}			61	
D_{71}		39		
D_{72}			-44	
Pa				
Pa				
Pp				
Pp				
Sc				
Sc				
As			42	41
As			41	
Ps			41	
Ps				

Note: Study 1 includes 400 normal adults (Cattell, 1973). Study 2 includes 190 clinical patients (Cattell, 1973). Study 3 includes 214 university undergraduates (Kameoka, 1977). Study 4 includes 179 normal and clinical adult cases (Cattell, 1974). Decimal points have been omitted.

TABLE 3.3 (Continued)

	H				I				L				M				N				O			
	1	2	3	4	1	2	3	4	1	2	3	4	1	2	3	4	1	2	3	4	1	2	3	4
A_1												51												
A_2																								
B_1													−36								−36			
B_2																								
C_1																43								
C_2																								
E_1																								
E_2																								
F_1		36																						
F_2						38				51													33	
G_1																								
G_2																								
H_1	66	55	60	75																				
H_2	53	53		69																				
I_1					76	39	66	85																
I_2					43	67	44	87																
L_1	−38								42	53	51		55								31			
L_2									32	80	60													
M_1										44			46			90								
M_2													47	41	56	88								
N_1	35																71							
N_2	−43																							
O_1																		69	39	76	48	58	47	80
O_2																		30	38	77	40	54	42	75
Q_{11}																			39					

Q_{12}

Q_{21}

Q_{22}

Q_{31}

Q_{32}

Q_{41}

Q_{42}

D_{11} 40

D_{12}

D_{21}

D_{22}

D_{31}

D_{32} 41

D_{41} − 33

D_{42} 44

D_{51} 54

D_{52} 42

D_{61}

D_{62}

D_{71}

D_{72}

Pa

Pa

Pp

Pp

Sc

Sc

As

As   − 35

Ps

Ps

TABLE 3.3 (Continued)

	Q₁				Q₂				Q₃				Q₄				D₁				D₂			
	1	2	3	4	1	2	3	4	1	2	3	4	1	2	3	4	1	2	3	4	1	2	3	4
A_1																								
A_2													45					−37				52		
B_1																								
B_2	54																							
C_1																				83				
C_2																	−40			40				
C_2																	−40			40				
E_1																	30							
E_2				−41																				
F_1					31												−43							
F_2									31															
G_1																				31				
G_2																								
H_1																	41							
H_2					−51						−30													
I_1																								
I_2													33	34										
L_1																								
L_2																								
M_1							−35														33			
M_2																								
N_1																								
N_2																								
O_1																								
O_2													36	54										
Q_{11}	62	39	41	85																				

Variable	Factor loadings / coefficients
Q_{12}	40
Q_{21}	61
Q_{22}	60
Q_{31}	76
Q_{32}	61, 68, 60, 66, 46, 58, 74, 73
Q_{41}	42
Q_{42}	61, 39, 66, 67, 47, 50, 85, 92, 50, 48, 39, 49, 39, 49, 89, 70
D_{11}	37
D_{12}	42, 65, 66, 93, 39, 57
D_{21}	32, 75, 48, 57
D_{22}	43, 75, 48, 88
D_{31}	
D_{32}	48, 75, 44, 88
D_{41}	42
D_{42}	
D_{51}	42, 43
D_{52}	
D_{61}	
D_{62}	38
D_{71}	41, −35
D_{72}	40
Pa	
Pa	
Pp	
Pp	
Sc	
Sc	36
As	38
As	40
Ps	37
Ps	38

TABLE 3.3 (Continued)

	D_3 1	2	3	4	D_4 1	2	3	4	D_5 1	2	3	4	D_6 1	2	3	4	D_7 1	2	3	4
A_1																				
A_2									30				34		32					
B_1																				
B_2																				
C_1													−40			−40				
C_2																69				
C_2																				
E_1						43			31											
E_2																				
F_1			58	70								33								
F_2				70		31														
G_1																				
G_2																				
H_1																40				
H_2																35				
I_1																				
I_2							39		37		54					32				
L_1																			41	66
L_2																				45
M_1																				
M_2																				
N_1																				
N_2																				
O_1																				
O_2													30							
Q_{11}							−42													

Q_{12}																				
Q_{21}																				
Q_{22}																				
Q_{31}																				
Q_{32}																	43			
Q_{41}													43							
Q_{42}																				
D_{11}										35						– 30				
D_{12}																72				
D_{21}																				
D_{22}																				
D_{31}	74	60	74	79									– 31				40	– 51		
D_{32}	76	53	54	69																
D_{41}					30	33	30	82												
D_{42}								82												
D_{51}									36	47	56	62					42			
D_{52}									35	58	51	76								
D_{61}												48	36	36	61	34				
D_{62}											30	32	35	58		33				
D_{71}																	33	42	61	73
D_{72}																	21	45	37	57
Pa																				
Pa																				
Pp														45						
Pp																				
Sc	52													35				30		
Sc	46	48								32										
As																				
As																				
Ps																				
Ps																				

TABLE 3.3 (*Continued*)

	Pa				Pp				Sc				As				Ps			
	1	2	3	4	1	2	3	4	1	2	3	4	1	2	3	4	1	2	3	4
A_1																				
A_2					45				-31				-30	-31			-30			
B_1																				
B_2																				
C_1							30													
C_2																				
C_2																				
E_1		31					48									36				
E_2																-32				
F_1					30															
F_2									40											
G_1																				
G_2																				
H_1														-52						
H_2														46						
I_1					-33															33
I_2																				
L_1																				
L_2																				
M_1													-30							
M_2						-49														
N_1	30																			
N_2																				
O_1													-31							
O_2																				

Q_{11}	45										
Q_{12}	61										
Q_{21}	38	62	69								
Q_{22}	56	68	80								
Q_{31}											
Q_{32}	42										
Q_{41}											
Q_{42}											
D_{11}											
D_{12}											
D_{21}	31										
D_{22}	32										
D_{31}	55	49	60	64							
D_{32}	61	44	62								
D_{41}	37		31								
D_{42}	-32			34							
D_{51}	32										
D_{52}		32				32					
D_{61}						-51					
D_{62}					36		39				
D_{71}	32										
D_{72}							43				
Pa				65							
Pa											
Pp							59				
Pp	33										
Sc	27	34	83	29	29	73	64	45			
Sc	45	58	77	27	52	50	67	56			
As	72								31	70	55	31
As	52								30	59	32	49
Ps			-34						-30		
Ps										-30	-32	71	47

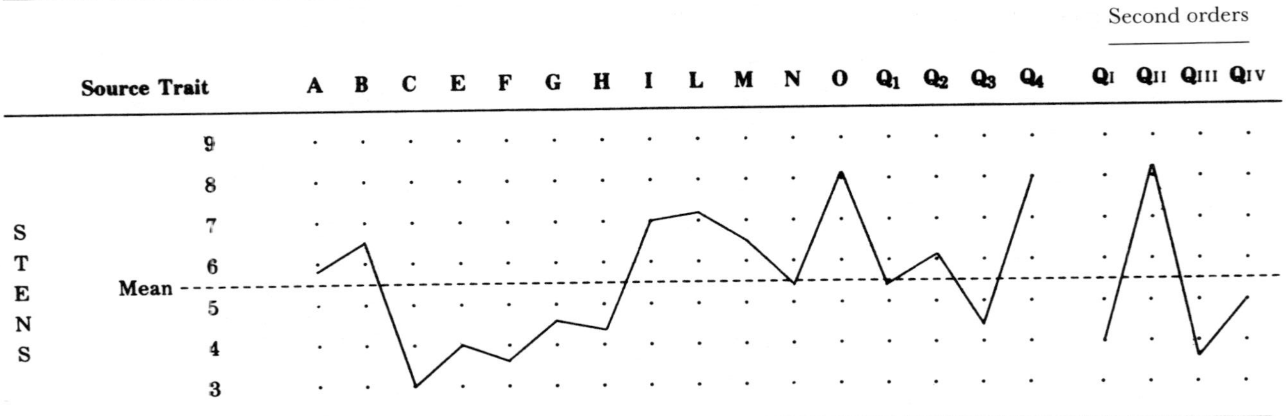

	A	B	C	E	F	G	H	I	L	M	N	O	Q_1	Q_2	Q_3	Q_4	Q_I	Q_{II}	Q_{III}	Q_{IV}
M ——	5.8	6.5	3.0	4.0	3.6	4.6	4.3	7.0	7.2	6.5	5.4	8.1	5.4	6.1	4.4	8.0	4.0	8.2	3.6	5.0
σ	2.1	2.0	2.3	2.1	2.1	2.0	2.4	2.0	2.3	2.1	2.0	2.5	1.5	1.7	2.1	2.3				

Notes: **This profile is based on data from 272 males and females.**

FIGURE 3.1 General neurotic profile. From *Handbook for the Sixteen Personality Factor Questionnaire (16PF)* (p. 265) by R. B. Cattell, H. W. Eber, and M. M. Tatsuoka. Champaign, IL, 1970. © 1970 Institute for Personality and Ability Testing. Reprinted by permission.

Source Trait	N	A	B	C	E	F	G	H	I	L	M	N	O	Q₁	Q₂	Q₃	Q₄		Q_I	Q_II	Q_III	Q_IV
																					Second orders		

Source Trait	N	A	B	C	E	F	G	H	I	L	M	N	O	Q_1	Q_2	Q_3	Q_4	Q_I	Q_{II}	Q_{III}	Q_{IV}
Antisocial Personality M	97	5.3	5.6	4.5	4.6	5.1	4.7	4.6	6.1	6.0	5.5	5.1	6.8	4.7	6.3	5.6	6.4	4.6	6.6	4.9	4.9
σ		1.9	1.9	2.5	1.9	1.9	2.1	2.0	2.0	2.3	1.9	1.9	2.6	2.0	1.8	2.0	2.5				
Criminals M	891	5.6	4.5	3.6	4.9	4.5	4.5	5.5	6.4	6.3	6.9	5.2	6.9	5.4	6.1	4.8	6.6	4.8	6.9	4.6	5.6
σ		1.8	3.0	2.4	2.0	2.3	2.1	1.9	2.3	2.0	2.2	2.2	1.8	1.7	1.7	2.1	2.0				
Sex Crime Convicts M	35	4.8	3.8	3.1	4.5	4.2	4.9	5.1	6.5	7.0	6.7	5.6	7.1	5.2	5.3	5.4	6.6	4.5	7.2	4.4	5.1
Psychopaths M	15	6.6	5.4	5.9	9.4	7.3	2.5	8.1	5.3	5.5	6.1	4.7	5.4	5.0	4.9	5.2	7.3	8.1	5.8	6.9	7.6
Exhibitionists M	38	5.5	4.7	3.8	5.8	4.8	4.7	4.9	5.5	6.7	6.4	5.5	7.4	6.5	6.5	4.7	7.3	4.8	7.3	5.1	6.0
σ		1.7	2.9	2.5	2.7	2.0	2.1	2.8	2.5	2.5	2.1	1.7	2.3	2.0	1.7	2.4	2.3				
Gang Delinquents M	45	5.7	4.5	4.6	6.2	6.3	4.6	5.6	6.0	6.2	5.6	5.9	5.5	4.9	5.0	4.1	6.7	6.1	6.5	5.5	5.5
Delinquents M	1728	5.4	4.3	5.5	6.1	5.6	5.3	5.5	5.0				5.3		5.5	4.8	5.2	5.9	5.6	6.2	5.7

Notes: The last profile, Delinquents, and the profile for Antisocial Personality are based on data from combined samples of males and females. All other profiles are based on data from male samples alone.

FIGURE 3.2 Antisocial behavior. From *Handbook for the Sixteen Personality Factor Questionnaire (16 PF)* (p. 279) by R. B. Cattell, H. W. Eber, and M. M. Tatsuoka. Champaign, IL, 1970. © 1970 Institute for Personality and Ability Testing. Reprinted by permission.

37

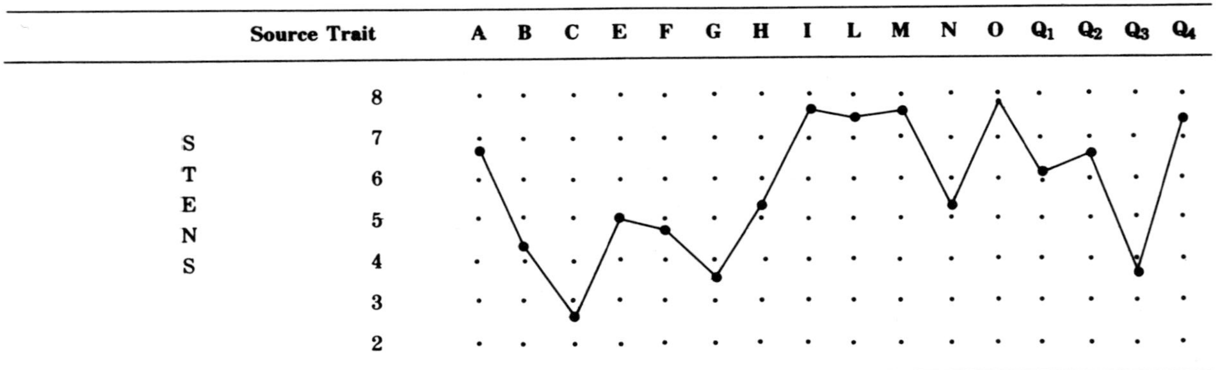

	N		A	B	C	E	F	G	H	I	L	M	N	O	Q_1	Q_2	Q_3	Q_4
Homosexuals (Australia)	**133**	**M** ·····	**6.6**	**4.2**	**2.6**	**5.0**	**4.8**	**3.6**	**5.3**	**7.6**	**7.3**	**7.7**	**5.3**	**7.9**	**6.1**	**6.6**	**4.8**	**7.4**
		σ	**2.4**	**2.0**	**1.8**	**2.4**	**2.2**	**1.7**	**2.7**	**2.1**	**2.0**	**1.9**	**2.5**	**2.1**	**2.2**	**2.1**	**2.3**	**1.9**

FIGURE 3.3 Homosexuals (133 male cases). From *Handbook for the Sixteen Personality Factor Questionnaire (16 PF)* (p. 265) by R. B. Cattell, H. W. Eber and M. M. Tatsuoka. Champaign, IL, 1970. © 1970 Institute for Personality and Ability Testing. Reprinted by permission.

the O–A battery, which are harder, and take longer, to administer, but which give excellent separation of depressives and neurotics from normals. They also aid, by discriminant function weights on the ten factors, in diagnosing the pathologies of the DSM III. The ten O–A factors include anxiety, regression, superego, exuberance, extraversion-invia, etc.; measures of the first two have been shown to change significantly with therapy and chemotherapy (Cattell, Rickels, et al., 1966). The O–A battery came out comparatively recently, and much remains to be found out about it as a monitoring device (Cattell & Schuerger, 1978).

Nothing will be said here about the modality of cognitive ability measurement, except to point out that where needed (schools and jobs) there are (a) batteries for both *fluid* (g_f) and *crystallized* (g_c) general intelligence and (b) *the Comprehensive Ability Battery* (CAB) for sixteen distinct *primary* abilities. The crystallized intelligence measure is available in the Wechsler Adult Intelligence Scale and the Wechsler Intelligence Scale for Children (WAIS and WISC); the fluid intelligence, in the three Culture Fair (CFIQ) 1970 scales for different age ranges. When the Culture Fair score is lower than the WAIS score, some indication of brain injury exists.

The CAB is an extension of the Thurstone primary ability scale from half-a-dozen to twenty demonstrated independent primaries (Hakstian and Cattell, 1976). It is used clinically to study brain injury, and, of course, in vocational guidance.

Finally, we come to the instrument of greatest use in clinical diagnosis and assessment — the MAT (Motivational Adjustment Test). Although this is a pencil-and-paper test, and can therefore be given in groups, it is objective, not a questionnaire. It uses the four best devices found through research on 100 objective motivation measurement devices, but the number of devices can be brought to six in individual testing situations by adding the Galvanic Skin Response (GSR) and reaction time.

As normally given, it measures the tension (arousal) level on five ergs — sex, fear, gregariousness, self-assertion, and narcism — and the activation level on five sems — sentiments to home, spouse or sweetheart, career, the self-sentiment, and the superego. (The last two serve as a check on the questionnaire measures.) Each of

Sten Mean I	DYNAMIC AREAS	STANDARD TEN SCORE (STEN) 1–10	Centile Rank U	Centile Rank I
4	CAREER SENTIMENT		77.3	22.7
4	HOME–PARENTAL SENTIMENT		40.1	22.7
7	FEAR ERG		59.9	77.3
5	NARCISM–COMFORT ERG		40.1	40.1
4	SUPEREGO SENTIMENT		77.3	22.7
4	SELF– SENTIMENT		59.9	22.7
5	MATING ERG		40.1	40.1
5	PUGNACITY–SADISM ERG		40.1	40.1
4	ASSERTIVENESS ERG		22.7	22.7
4	SWEETHEART–SPOUSE SENTIMENT		40.1	22.7

Integrated Sten Mean -----   Integrated Sten Mean ———

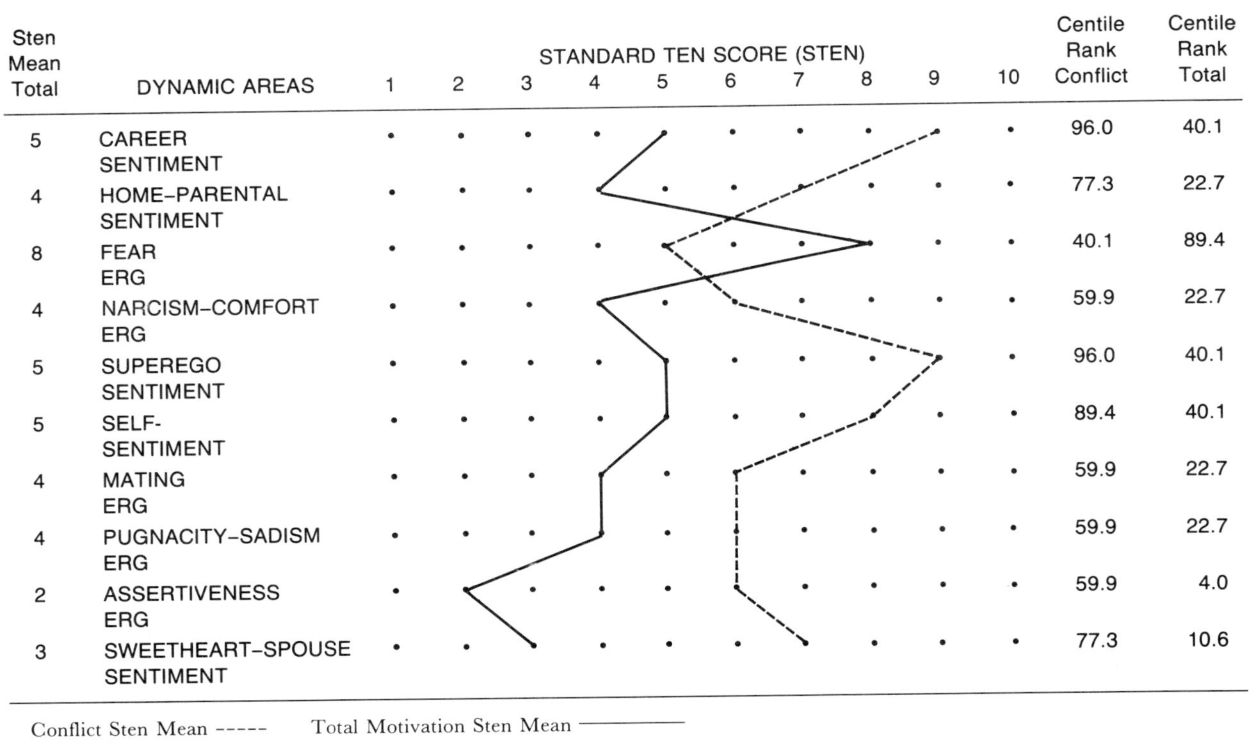

Sten Mean Total	DYNAMIC AREAS	STANDARD TEN SCORE (STEN)	Centile Rank Conflict	Centile Rank Total
5	CAREER SENTIMENT		96.0	40.1
4	HOME–PARENTAL SENTIMENT		77.3	22.7
8	FEAR ERG		40.1	89.4
4	NARCISM–COMFORT ERG		59.9	22.7
5	SUPEREGO SENTIMENT		96.0	40.1
5	SELF-SENTIMENT		89.4	40.1
4	MATING ERG		59.9	22.7
4	PUGNACITY–SADISM ERG		59.9	22.7
2	ASSERTIVENESS ERG		59.9	4.0
3	SWEETHEART–SPOUSE SENTIMENT		77.3	10.6

Conflict Sten Mean – – – –   Total Motivation Sten Mean ——

FIGURE 3.4 Motivational patterns of the chronically unemployed. (F. Lawlis, 1967) $N = 75$. From *Individual Assessment with the Motivation Analysis Test* (p. 24) by A. B. Sweney. Champaign, IL, 1969. © 1969 Institute for Personality and Ability Testing, Inc. Reprinted by permission.

these measures has two components — an *integrated* component, *I*, from information and word association; and an *unintegrated* or unconscious component, *U*, from the projection and the autism subtests. Figure 3.4 illustrates with the *U* and the *I* scores of a group of chronically unemployed at a rehabilitation center.

The scoring of the MAT is somewhat complicated due to having to combine separately calculated *U* and *I* standard scores; but much more can be derived from it than the simple levels of tension and satisfaction of the drives. Clinicians find the difference of *U* and *I* scores very significant for estimating areas of major conflict. If the unconscious, *U*, score for, say, sex, is much higher than the integrated, *I*, score, one finds that there has been environmental suppression of normal expression, and that conflict therefore exists. The MAT can be machine scored, like the other tests above, with supplied programs.

The nature and implications of levels on the *general personality* factors (in the 16 PF) and the *dynamic structure* factors (the MAT and SMAT) will be already known to most psychologists, but the next chapter will interpret them in the clinical context.[3]

NOTE

[3]Very adequate accounts of the meanings of the 28 general and pathological source traits in the CAQ and 16 PF are available in Heather Cattell's writings (1983, 1984), in Karson & O'Dell (1976), in the Handbooks for the tests, and in countless articles. The clinician is strongly urged to acquire a refined conception of their meanings for a full interpretation and understanding of his or her clinical cases.

Chapter 4

The Measures Interpreted in the Context of Clinical Cases

Let us consider the case of a 17-year-old boy referred for constant truancy from school. His 16 PF and MAT profiles are as shown in Figure 4.1.

It will be seen at once that on the 16 PF he is of exceptionally high intelligence, of reasonably good ego strength, low on boldness, H, and high on both dominance, E, and protension, L. He is also rather low on self-sentiment, Q_3, and affectia, A. On the MAT he is high on narcism, low on self-sentiment and home attachment, and, strangely, high on career interest.

In discussion the boy explained that he was bored with school work, that it was below his intelligence level, and that he had few friends in class (a low H characteristic). He had resisted his parents' efforts to get him to attend school regularly, and he spent his time reading, mainly technical magazines. The combination of low H (shyness) with high intelligence, and high E and L, which enable him firmly to rationalize his behavior to himself, tells most of the story. The combination of shyness with dominance is unusual, but easily possible, and results in obstinacy, sometimes issuing in paranoid behavior. The MAT results bear out the low self-sentiment, showing, by a higher U than I component, that he has been frustrated in building up his self-concept (identity). They also show a high I score on the fear erg.

The "collusion" of these traits in leading to his behavior is reasonably clear. He is too narcistic and shy to make friends readily,

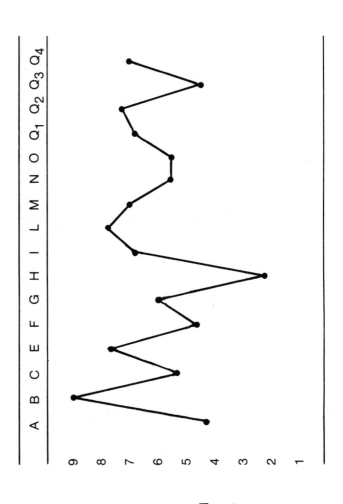

44

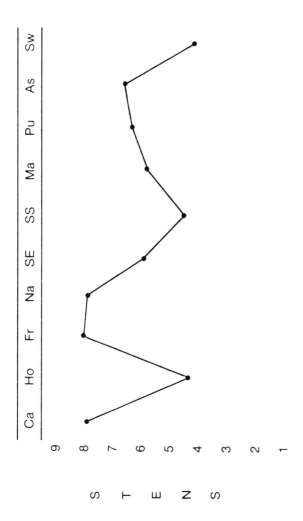

FIGURE 4.1 16 PF (*top*) and MAT (*bottom*) profiles of boy truant.

and his high E (dominance) and L (protension) factors strengthen
the pose of "superiority" that his high intelligence enables him to
assume. He has a substantial social problem with his peers, in addition to his purely educational problem, because of being placed
in a grade distinctly lower than his mental age indicates.

We would thus see his withdrawal and truant behavior analyzed
in the behavioral equation as follows, using estimates of the b's:

$$\text{Clinical problem} = .3A + .5B - .2C + .3E - .6H + .4L - .4Q_3$$

$$+ .3 \text{ (narcism, from MAT)}$$

$$- .3 \text{ (parental home, from MAT)} \qquad (4.1)$$

If these weights are applied to the trait scores for A, B, C, and
so forth in the profile above, we get a standard score of the "symptom" of 7.2, which is indeed "way out." Incidentally, the difference
in direction in weighting of Q_3 (the self-esteem sem) and of the
narcism is seen as the result of the mother's ignoring the child, causing him to be arrested at the attempt to give himself bodily com-
fort, as the test items on narcism show. The self-image and its attitudes in Q_3, on the other hand, are a much later growth of desire
for social approval of the self, bringing on attitudes of social con-
formity and preservation of an undamaged self-object. These two
measures scarcely correlate (Figure 4.1), and whereas Q_3 pulls
against the unpopular symptom behavior, narcism ["plus" sign in
equation (4.1)] aids it.

According to our basic analysis, in treatment we first have to
change the b's (loadings) that make his social "stand-offishness" so
powerful. Secondly, we have to work on the traits that we know
are amenable to change—E, L, Q_3, the erg of narcism, and the
sem to home (H and A, we know from genetic research, are highly
inheritable components in introversion, and will change relatively
little.)

As an external manipulation, we arranged to have the boy raised
to the next higher school class grade. (His absences had scarcely
affected his academic achievement.) He expressed gratitude for this
and found the new position satisfying. The attempted adjustment

of trait involvements — the *b*'s — had to proceed initially through consulting-room, cognitively pursued insights. He was brought to see the personality motives for his social rejection, particularly his dominance and his narcistic self-involvement. Motivated by his total desire to remove the symptom, he sat in a chair and rehearsed with the therapist new ways of expressing his interest in others, and similarly gained insight and control over other traits. He discussed his self sem image in Q_3, especially what he wanted to be on leaving school, and he built up a more effective guiding image, with the warm aid of the therapist. His progress in actual behaviors in daily contacts was examined and approved and modified. There was a shift, shown possible in research, of endowment from narcism to the self sem. In discussions, the preoccupation of the individual with himself (narcism) was transferred to a growth of self-approved values in the self-sentiment. The result was, in six months, a relatively well-adjusted 18-year-old, with recordable changes on the monitoring re-test on the traits to be manipulated.

A second case, with monitoring by retests on the MAT, is that of a middle-aged alcoholic, with general problems with his job and his family. His first test, on arrival, on the MAT, is shown in Figure 4.2.

The interview confirmed in detail his high fear, connected with possibly losing his job, as well as a constant anger (pugnacity), the source of which he could not place. What also fitted closely into specific behaviors was his lack of interest in his life purposes ("all absorbed now in drink"), as shown in low unintegrated interest in wife and mating (he had become impotent), low career interest, and low superego and low self-assertion. The interpretation of MAT scores requires less specialized knowledge than that of 16 PF and CAQ factors, some traits of which, especially beyond *A*, *B*, and *C*, are unfamiliar to anyone who has not studied the factor analytic discoveries (see the Handbooks). By contrast the ergs in MAT are fully familiar to each of us by emotional experience (sex, fear, gregariousness, etc.) and the sems are also common properties in the meaning of attachment to parents, to job, to the self-image, and so forth.

In the case of the profile on the MAT in Figure 4.2, the treat-

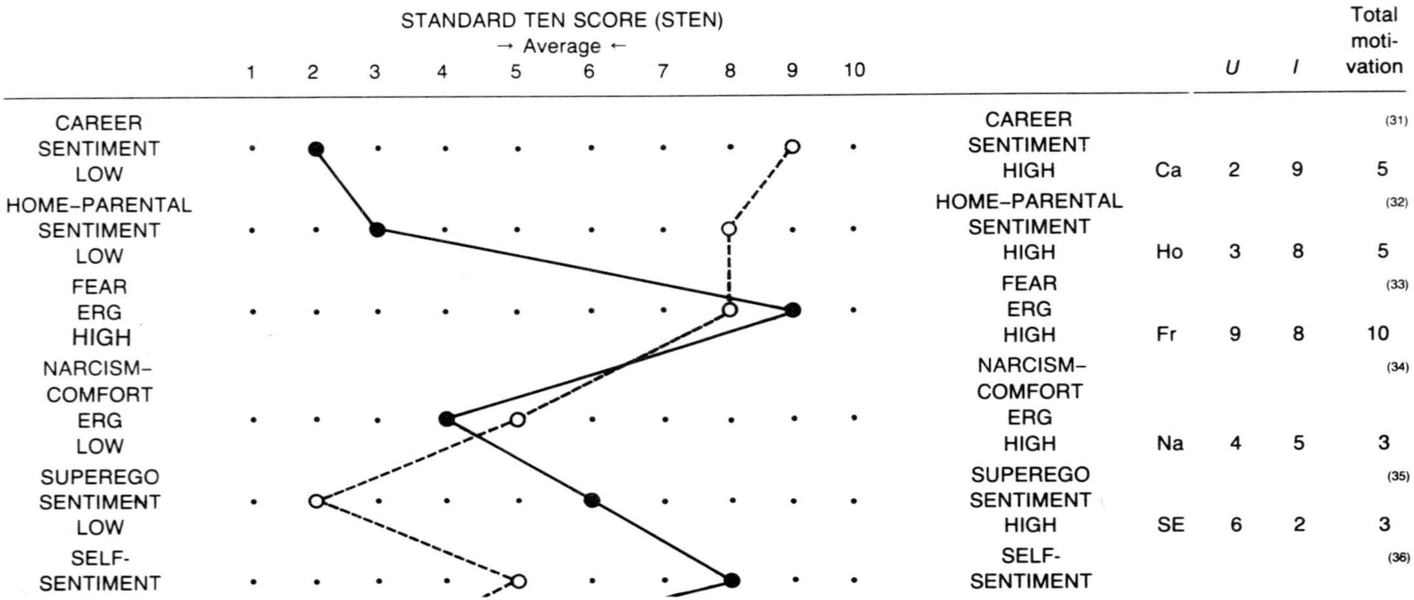

STANDARD TEN SCORE (STEN)

→ Average ←

1　2　3　4　5　6　7　8　9　10

			Total moti-vation
	U	I	
CAREER SENTIMENT HIGH	Ca	2	9	(31) 5
HOME-PARENTAL SENTIMENT HIGH	Ho	3	8	(32) 5
FEAR ERG HIGH	Fr	9	8	(33) 10
NARCISM-COMFORT ERG HIGH	Na	4	5	(34) 3
SUPEREGO SENTIMENT HIGH	SE	6	2	(35) 3
SELF-SENTIMENT				(36)

CAREER SENTIMENT LOW

HOME-PARENTAL SENTIMENT LOW

FEAR ERG HIGH

NARCISM-COMFORT ERG LOW

SUPEREGO SENTIMENT LOW

SELF-SENTIMENT

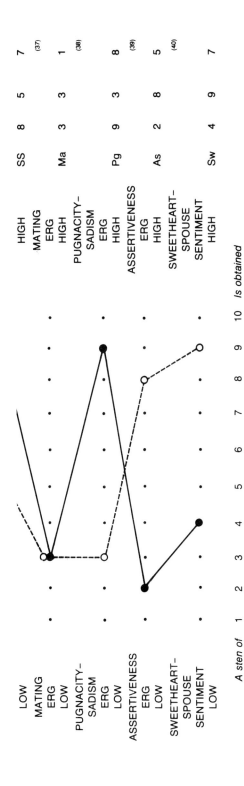

FIGURE 4.2 Mr Y. First MAT profile. $U(\bullet)$, $I(\bigcirc)$, and total scores on all ten factors. From Cattell and Johnson (1985) with permission.

STANDARD TEN SCORE (STEN)
← Average →

1 2 3 4 5 6 7 8 9 10

	U	I	Total motivation
Ca	5	7	7
Ho	7	9	10
Fr	4	6	5
Na	5	7	7
SE	4	7	5

CAREER SENTIMENT HIGH / LOW
HOME-PARENTAL SENTIMENT HIGH / LOW
FEAR ERG HIGH / LOW
NARCISM-COMFORT ERG HIGH / LOW
SUPEREGO SENTIMENT HIGH / LOW
SELF-SENTIMENT

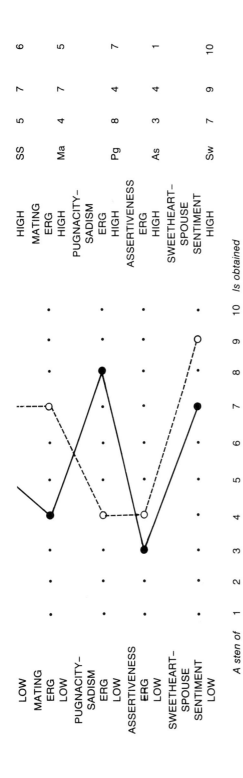

A sten of 1 2 3 4 5 6 7 8 9 10 Is obtained
by about 2.3% 4.4% 9.2% 15.0% 19.1% 19.1% 15.0% 9.2% 4.4% 2.3% of adults

FIGURE 4.3 Mr Y. Second MAT profile. $U(●)$, $I(○)$, and total scores on all ten factors. From Cattell and Johnson (1986) with permission.

ment plan (H. Cattell, 1984, 1986) consisted of two phases. The initial phase, which took place in a residential alcoholism treatment facility and lasted 6 weeks, was designed to (1) assist him to gain insight into his underlying dynamics, (2) increase his awareness of alcoholism as a progressive physical and emotional disorder, (3) introduce him to Alcoholics Anonymous, as a support system, (4) help him acquire interference and self-management (ego strength) skills, and (5) facilitate healing of the strained relations within his family, i.e., rebuild the sem to the wife.

The second phase, following release, lasted 4½ months, during which he lived at home and resumed his former employment. During this time he came for therapeutic interviews and AA meetings. The first MAT had indicated apathy, a sense of failure in career, fear and anxiety, guilt, low self-esteem (Q_3), and so forth. The final MAT profile, at the end of treatment, in Figure 4.3, indicates decided changes, all in a satisfactory direction — except for the angry pugnacity and the assertiveness scores. He has regained an average score on sex and a decidedly more than average attachment to his wife. Fear is in the normal range, as also is career. Regarding the latter, and in keeping with his assertiveness reduction, he has abandoned the ambitious struggle toward eminence in his job, the stress of which had been one of the major pressures forcing him into alcoholism. Also there is an upward change in narcism, with relaxations and pleasures that, at least temporarily, aid in providing substitutes for alcohol. The therapist decided that some basic persistence in the pugnacity score must spring from the patient's expressed dissatisfaction with parental treatment in childhood. The patient's sobriety and new satisfactions in his job persisted in a retest a year after the conclusion of treatment.[4]

In view of the social importance of the personality change in a whole group, recently speculated to occur in Vietnam war veterans, the data (courtesy of Cagley and Savage, 1984) (see Figure 4.4) is of interest.

Although this is *difference* data, it seems reasonable to attribute it to change, because the control group matching is so good. Neither the veterans nor the ex-servicemen not in the war showed any difference on cognitive ability profiles or on 14 of the 16 normal traits in the CAQ (the 16 PF); it is reasonable to assume that the marked

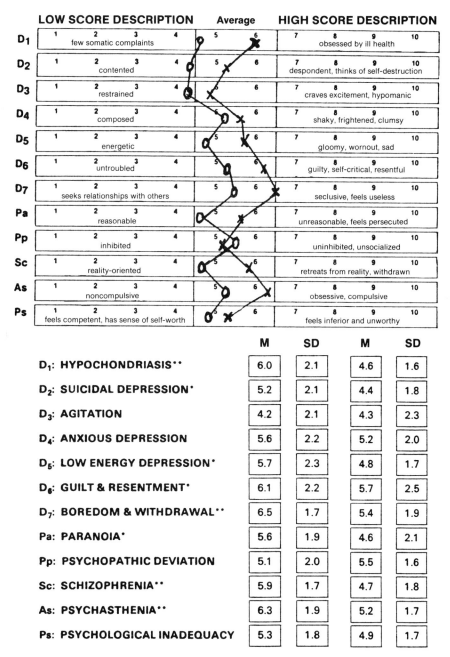

LOW SCORE DESCRIPTION	Average	HIGH SCORE DESCRIPTION

	M	SD	M	SD
D_1: HYPOCHONDRIASIS**	6.0	2.1	4.6	1.6
D_2: SUICIDAL DEPRESSION*	5.2	2.1	4.4	1.8
D_3: AGITATION	4.2	2.1	4.3	2.3
D_4: ANXIOUS DEPRESSION	5.6	2.2	5.2	2.0
D_5: LOW ENERGY DEPRESSION*	5.7	2.3	4.8	1.7
D_6: GUILT & RESENTMENT*	6.1	2.2	5.7	2.5
D_7: BOREDOM & WITHDRAWAL**	6.5	1.7	5.4	1.9
Pa: PARANOIA*	5.6	1.9	4.6	2.1
Pp: PSYCHOPATHIC DEVIATION	5.1	2.0	5.5	1.6
Sc: SCHIZOPHRENIA**	5.9	1.7	4.7	1.8
As: PSYCHASTHENIA**	6.3	1.9	5.2	1.7
Ps: PSYCHOLOGICAL INADEQUACY	5.3	1.8	4.9	1.7

FIGURE 4.4 Differences of stressed (*left*) and unstressed (*right*) military veterans. *Difference significant at $p < .05$. **Difference significant at $p < .01$. X, Australian Vietnam Veterans (AVV). O, Australian Ex-Servicemen (AES). Courtesy of Drs. J. M. Cagley and R. D. Savage (*Australian Journal of Psychology*, 1964).

differences in the abnormal traits in the CAQ in Figure 4.4 (notably on hypochondriasis, suicidal depression, low energy depression, withdrawal, schizophrenic tendency, and psychasthenia (compulsiveness) are well measured by the test. This pattern constitutes what the psychologists call "psychological stress syndrome" (occurring up to ten years after the event).

NOTE

⁴See account of this case in H. Cattell (1986).

Chapter 5

The More Precise Meaning of the Involvement Indices and Modulators: b's, v's, and s's

In the model, we have so far kept close to the meanings for the b's as derived from simple multiple experimental research. They are the factor loadings (which are also the beta weights) of traits obtained for the given, measured criterion behavior.[5] They can be both positive and negative — positive when a trait helps the performance, as intelligence does academic achievement; negative when increase in the trait impedes the performance, as increase in dominance impedes some social learning.

However, structured learning theory shows that these b's are the outcomes of several influences and can be further broken down and analyzed into meaningful components. In the first place the ambient situation, k, can to some extent *modify the level of the trait itself, before the trait goes into action*. By the ambient situation (k) we mean the general life situation in which the stimulus (h) is met. For example, a person would respond differently to the stimulus of an examination paper in a cool room than in a hot, stuffy room. Or an alcoholic might respond differently to the offer of a drink from his therapist and from a group of his buddies.

The effect of ambient situations, represented by k's in the behavioral equation, is considerable and is studied experimentally by *modulation theory*. The effect of modulation on personality components is most evident in personality *states*, but has been shown also to operate to a lesser degree on *traits*. The level of factors E (dominance) and F (surgency) are modified, for example, by an atmosphere of group admiration, and of group freedom of atmosphere, respectively.

The way to represent this change in the behavioral equation is by a modulation index, s_{xk}, which says how much, for the average person, the state x is changed in the ambient situation k. Typically we write:

$$S_{xki} = s_{xk}L_{xi} \qquad (5.1)$$

This says that the level of the state S_x, in person i, in situation k is fixed by multiplying his personal liability, L_{xi}—(proneness) to the given state, x—by the modulator s_{xk} for that state in that situation, k (for ordinary people).

So far we have not used states (S's) in any of the previous behavioral equations, but as our model moves closer to reality we have to recognize that the psychological state—e.g., anxiety or anger—that a person is in will sometimes affect behavior more than the traits. The *full* behavioral equation in fact has traits *and* states, as follows:

$$a_{hijk} = \sum^{x=p} b_{hjkx} T_{xi} + \sum^{s=q} b_{hjks} S_{si} \qquad (5.2)$$

As we move to more complete equations we shall increasingly use the Σ sign, which means "summed across" all the contributors of a given kind. In the above equation, the first term sums across all p traits (as shown by $x = p$) and all q states ($s - q$), which combine to estimate the final result in performance response, a_{hijk}. The states are, of course, general states, like anxiety, arousal, depression, and fatigue, which can be measured by the Cattell–Curran 8-State Questionnaire[6] (shown, in second-order structure, in Table 6.3), and specific ergic states, like fear, lust, and anger (that are measured as part of what is measured in the MAT and SMAT). Thus we might write a full equation for a person meeting the stimulus, h, of a locked door in running out of the situation, k, of a house on fire, thus:

$$a_{hijk} = v_{hjx}s_{kx}L_{xi} + v_{hjy}s_{ky}L_{yi} + \cdots v_{hjp}s_{kp}L_{pi} \qquad (5.3)$$

(state contribution only) where a_{hjk} is the force used in breaking down (j) the door (h) in the situation of the house on fire (k). Here, L_{xi} might be i's liability (proneness) to the emotion of fear; L_{yi} might be his liability to rage. The modulators s_{ks} and s_{ky} are the typical degree to which fear and rage are evoked in the "house on fire" situation, k. The v values are the remainder of the discovered b values when the s_k's are taken out of them. They give the involvements (the contributions of states S_x and S_y) to the violence of action. Thus we ask both (1) how much does the situation provoke the state (or trait) in size (s_k) and (2) how much does that state at that size reinforce the behavior (v_{hj}).

The separate criterion validities of state measures of anxiety, stress, anger, etc., have not been fully provided for in most presently available tests (but see Cattell and Johnson, 1984). However, Cattell and Brennan (1986) have shown that the modulation model works, and that both state liabilities, L's, for an individual and state modulators, s's, can be calculated. The s's can be obtained factor analytically from factoring the *same* performance for the *same* people in *different* situations. If we suppose, as the model does, that the obtained b's can then be broken down into a v (an involvement term that says how much the trait, whatever its level, is involved in raising the performance) and that the s determines the state (or trait) level, then we have the alternative of additive or product action of v and s to give the obtained b, thus:

$$b_{jk} = v_j s_k \text{ or } b_{jk} = (v_j + s_k) \qquad (5.4)$$

The former seems easier for calculations and we shall adopt it. Thus:

$$b_{hjkx}S_{xi} = v_{hjx}s_{kx}L_{xi} \qquad (5.5)$$

In these formulae for the behavioral equation it is usually assumed to be R-technique (i.e., calculated on a sample of people), and the s_k's are then the *average* effect on all people in the given ambient situation. For example, breaking down a resistant door in a house on fire would for most people have a large s_k on the fear erg, while resting on a beach would have a small s_k. However, there are occasions when (since s_k's would vary somewhat according to a person's past experience) accurate values for s_k's would need to be obtained individually by longitudinal P-technique experiment.

The s_k's will mainly express the provocation of emotional states, though, as Horn has shown (1972), even the two intelligences, g_f and g_c, vary slightly from situation to situation, and should ideally have an s_k term additional to the weight for their involvement, v_{hj}, in the performance. However, the main s_k weights appear in the *dynamic* traits, and we see that they must arise either from previous learning or from innate nervous connections. Thus, if a situation, such as a sexual situation, has both innate, n, and acquired, a, effects on an erg, E, then we should write:

$$E_{knai} = (s_{knx} + s_{kax})\, E_{xi} \qquad (5.6)$$

to settle the level of arousal E_{knai}. That is to say, we can speak of both innate and learned parts operating in the total provocative situation.

The origins of ergic arousal levels thus theoretically reside in two parts of the situation, but probably in most civilized life situations we can look largely to conditioning (to coexcitation and means–end learning in the five principles in Chapter 1) for the origins of the modulation value. It follows that if we deal with relatively stable individuals in a relatively stable, long-experienced environment, then the s_k's tell us how much provocation and satisfaction the situation k has *habitually* given to the dynamic trait concerned.

This contribution of s_k's to tell us ultimately about measures of *satisfaction* gained in the situation needs discussion. There can be debate about this meaning of the acquired s_k's, since some will argue that their size indicates how much the situation *arouses* the erg, rather than how much it *satisfies* it. We must distinguish between a first experience, when the s_k is indeed the provocation, regardless of satisfaction, and the later experience, when an erg is aroused only to the extent that it is subsequently habitually satisfied. The reflexological law of *extinction* in an unsatisfied behavioral response operates to reduce the value of an initial s_k. This will depend partly on whether we speak of the *innate* s_{knx} in equation (5.6) above, or the *acquired* s_{kax}. When a piece of machinery roars past a man for the first time, his response is partly innate fear of the noise and partly perception (reasoned, acquired) of the real danger of being run over. With assurance that the second is not likely to happen (extinction procedure), the acquired trait loading (s_{kxa}) disappears but the innate response to the roar remains. Or, again, the maternal feeling of a woman to her baby would arise partly from an innate and partly from an acquired modulator, and these play different roles at different times.

The s_k part of the loading in habitual behavior is therefore an indication of how much real, habitual satisfaction of the given kind normally arises from the situation. Of course there are commonly, among s_k's, some *negative* loadings, which mean that the given course of action habitually *deprives* the individual of some satisfaction in that erg. As we shall discuss in Chapter 7, the individual often perseveres nevertheless in the course of action unsatisfying to an erg because it gives more positive satisfactions on other ergs.

Now the meaning of a situation — its perception — is defined basically by what the person *does* in response to it. The meaning of the satisfaction he gets from it is obviously representable quantitatively by the vector values of the series of s_k's for what he continually does in situation k. The full meaning includes also the involvement indices, the v's, saying what effects his drives and abilities have on the given performance. However, the v's define how much the traits contribute to the action, and define a cognitive rather than a dynamic, emotional meaning.

It follows that in the vectors of s's we have a means of precisely defining *the emotional meanings of situations*. By comparing the vector profiles of two situations by means of the pattern similarity coefficients, r_p, we can express just how similar they are. Work along these lines will eventually supply the clinician with the statements of the similarity of two situations in the satisfactions to be derived from them, and thus on the practicality of switching a patient from one to the other. Comparison in a matrix of r_p's of a large number of situations will permit them objectively to be gathered, by the Taxonome program, within "types of situations," that could be a valuable guide to logically arranging life adjustments.

A byproduct of the modulation model, incidentally, is that it can lead to a solution to one of the oldest problems in psychology — the provision of scales with absolute zeros, and therefore ratio scale units. This opens the way to many calculations not previously legitimately possible (Cattell and Brennan, 1986). Its greatest relevance to therapy, however, is in the ability it gives us, with some trivial increase in complication, to include state measures and situational meanings in our practice.

NOTES

[5]The statistically minded will recognize that the values of the b's, behavioral indices (which are factor loadings), are not *precisely* the same as the weights, w's, we give to each behavior in estimating the factor. But they are roughly similar, as the weights in an estimation equation are to the correlations of the behaviors with the criterion. The actual relation is (Cattell, 1978):

$$V_w = V_b R_v^{-1}$$

where V_w and V_b are the weight and index matrices and R_v^{-1} is the inverse of the correlations among the behaviors predictive of the trait level.

[6]This questionnaire battery contains scales for eight of the nine or ten states so far located by dR- and P-technique factorizations of change scores. The states are: (1) anxiety, (2) stress (frequently confused with anxiety but properly a physiological *effort* stress), (3) depression (capable of division into three secondary factors and seven primaries), (4) regression (a state of dismay and overwroughtness, of great clinical importance), (5) fatigue (general), (6) guilt, (7) extraversion (exvia–invia is a state as well

as a trait), and (8) arousal (instinctual general arousal in the limbic system).

There are substantial correlations among certain states (see Table 6.3), notably of .62 and .77 of anxiety with stress and depression, respectively, and of depression with regression (.75). There are broadly two second-order factors from these correlations, one covering anxiety, stress, depression, and guilt, and the other low arousal, depression, and fatigue (Boyle, 1983). It is unknown at present whether these correlations arise through correlation of situations, e.g., of frustration with suppression, or from inherent connections in the hypothalamus. (*Handbook of State Measurement*, 8SPQ test forms, answer sheets, and keys available from IPAT, Champaign, Illinois.

Chapter 6

The Organization of Trait and Type Measures in Diagnosis

Following the above incursion into the field of dynamic traits and states — to broaden concepts and introduce situations — we should now return to a deeper appreciation of the diagnosis of the individual now rendered possible.

The psychiatric *Diagnostic and Statistical Manual* (or DSM) uses the concept of *types*. A person is diagnosed by being assigned to a type, whence we think we gain some predictive power in regard to the course of his illness and its treatment. There is a fundamental difference that must be kept in mind between analysis by traits and assignment to a type. Unitary traits can be represented diagrammatically by coordinates, as in intelligence and anxiety in Figure 6.1.

Types are clusterings of people in a coordinate space, as shown by the three "balls" of dense points in Figure 6.1. The individuals in type 1 are simply intelligent people; those in type 2 are rather intelligent but also quite anxious; and those in type 3 are rather sluggish persons, with both low intelligence and low anxiety. Incidentally, a mistaken use of type lies in applying it to the extremes on a simple *dimension* (trait), e.g., extravert and introvert "types." This would make sense only if there were *not* more individuals in between the two clumps than in them; but almost invariably there are more in the middle — unclassifiable — than at the ends in regard to extraversion–introversion.

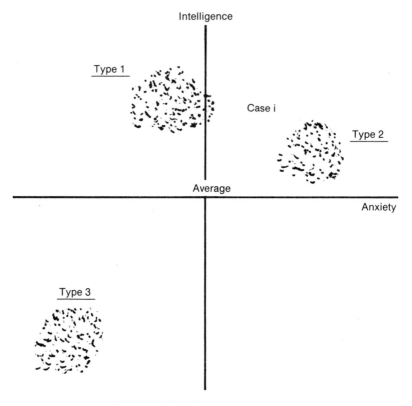

FIGURE 6.1 Traits and types.

There are two main objections to the use of type diagnosis: first, as stated, the word is used unnecessarily when *score on a dimension* would be more precise; second, there often *is* no type in existence corresponding to the verbal concept. That is to say, no one has shown that there exists a configuration of characteristics in individuals corresponding to the configurations that define, for example, unicorns or angels. (A recent false example is the "psychological type A" in heart disease.) The utility of a true type, as Aristotle used it, is that if we know — by scoring traits *a* through *d* — that a person belongs to a type, then we can infer that he will also have defined, in time, traits *e* through *g*. Thus diagnosis as a schizophrenic implies a resistance to treatment and a certain prolonged life course. The Renaissance brought on, in opposition to Aristotle, the Galilean device of measurement, and degrees of analyzed qualities, in a profile peculiar to the individual. Psychological diagnosis today is ready, by reason of analyzed, measurable traits, for a shift from the Aristotelian DSM and MMPI practices to the Galilean basis of general scientific analysis.

Types have demonstrable existence principally in disease — a person either is or is not a case of tuberculosis, typhoid fever, or schizophrenia. But the necessary work of sorting all existent profiles by the pattern similarity coefficient and the computer taxonome program (Cattell, Coulter, and Tsujioka, 1966) to discover what denser groups of configurations exist in behavioral space has not yet been done by psychiatrists. The categories of the DSM are decided by committees, not by scientific research with Taxonome principles applied to measured profiles. Nevertheless, we can grant at a commonsense level that such types exist as schizophrenics, manic depressives, anxiety hysterics, and some others.

As case conferences frequently have to admit, a case can be a mixed type. This can be rendered as a precise diagnosis by working out the distance — the pattern similarity — of the patient's profile to two or three central profiles of types. The situation can be seen by the distances of case i in Figure 6.1 from the center of existing clusters. (He belongs here as much to Type 2 as to Type 1.) However, as we have indicated, diagnosis by types is tied up with the "disease concept" of mental disorder, which a majority of practitioners are not altogether happy with. In any case, the psychologist is asked by the psychiatrist to help by testing the patient; and a number of signs have been picked up on the Rorschach, blindly, that do occur with one type more than another. However, since the mean trait profile has now been worked out on the 16 PF, CAQ, O-A battery, etc., for at least thirty alleged psychiatric, DSM types (Cattell, Eber, and Tatsuoka, 1970), it has become possible to assign a patient with greater reliability to a category via an r_p between the patient's profile and the disease category control profile, as shown in Figure 6.2.

The Galilean, modern scientific approach works out its conclu-

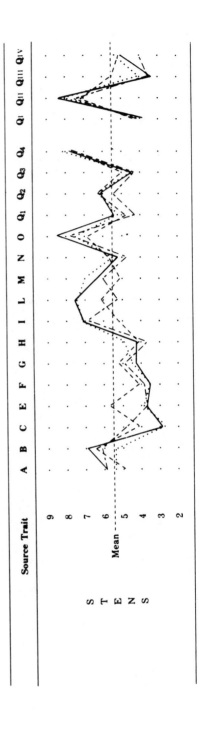

	N																					
Anxiety Reaction	80	M ——	5.9	6.9	2.8	3.7	3.5	4.3	4.3	7.1	7.5	6.4	5.2	8.5	5.4	6.1	4.5	7.8	3.8	8.3	3.4	5.0
		σ	2.1	2.0	2.3	2.1	2.1	2.4	1.9	2.3	2.3	2.3	2.1	2.6	1.5	1.9	2.3	2.5				
Conversion Reaction	31	M - - -	4.9	6.5	4.2	5.7	4.1	5.2	4.2	5.2	6.1	5.2	5.7	6.9	4.7	6.2	5.0	7.7	4.4	7.2	5.5	5.1
		σ	1.9	2.4	2.0	2.6	1.8	2.1	1.5	2.6	2.8	2.4	2.3	2.6	1.9	2.0	2.3	2.2				
Depressive Reaction	70	M ·····	5.4	5.4	2.7	3.9	3.5	4.5	4.9	7.1	7.4	7.0	5.5	7.5	5.2	6.2	4.5	8.1	4.0	8.0	4.1	5.3
		σ	2.1	1.8	2.2	2.1	1.9	1.5	2.6	1.8	2.2	1.8	1.9	2.1	1.5	1.3	1.5	2.0				
Obsessive Compulsive	29	M - · -	5.9	6.1	4.8	3.7	3.8	4.9	3.7	6.7	5.3	6.0	4.8	7.7	4.4	5.4	4.4	7.7	4.1	7.5	3.5	4.0
		σ	2.3	1.8	1.9	2.0	2.4	2.0	2.2	2.3	2.5	1.7	2.3	2.3	1.3	1.6	2.1	2.2				
Inadequate Personality	54	M	5.9	5.1	3.8	5.1	5.4	4.8	4.1	6.3	7.0	7.3	5.5	7.7	5.9	6.7	5.2	7.4	4.6	7.5	4.6	6.0
		σ	1.9	2.0	3.1	3.0	2.7	2.6	2.2	2.1	1.8	1.8	2.8	1.9	1.8	2.7	2.5	2.6				
Psychosomatic	76	M	5.2	6.9	4.9	5.3	4.8	5.0	5.1	5.5	4.7	5.6	6.4	6.2	4.2	6.2	5.1	6.8	4.9	6.5	5.6	4.8
		σ	1.9	2.6	2.0	2.0	1.7	2.2	2.8	1.2	2.3	2.4	2.3	3.4	2.1	2.1	2.2	2.0				

Notes: All profiles in this figure are based on combined male and female data.

FIGURE 6.2 Diagnostic DSM matching of an individual's profile. From Handbook for the *Sixteen Personality Factor Questionnaire (16 PF)* (p. 267) by R. B. Cattell, H. W. Eber, and M. M. Tatsuoka. Champaign, IL, 1970. © 1970 Institute for Personality and Ability Testing. Reprinted with permission.

sions more from the analytical trait measurements themselves. Except in the case of the psychotic, who often shows a specific disease type pattern, understanding and treatment by trait scores suits better the view that the patient is normal, in the sense that his disorder is a tangle in normal processes, albeit extreme or malfunctioning. Certainly this functional model applies to the vast majority of neurotics, drug addicts, and people unhappy in marriage or job who seek out psychotherapists.

This view calls upon us to make a deeper study of traits than in the introductory treatment in Chapter 3. Principally we must follow research into what in further factor analysis are called second-order, or *secondary*, factors. *Primary* factors, as in the CAQ, prove to be consistently moderately intercorrelated. For example (see Cattell, Eber, and Tatsuoka, 1970), factors A (affectia) and F (surgency) correlate around .35, while ego strength, C, and ergic tension, i.e., frustration, Q_4, can reach -50.

From a correlation matrix among the primaries one can factor analyze to get at the causes or patterns *beyond* the primaries. The typical result (incidentally, checked across countries) is as shown in Table 6.1.

Since there is an as yet inexplicable variation of patterns among samples on the secondaries IV and V, we will confine ourselves to the rest. Factor I proves to be *exvia–invia* — the name given to the precise core in extraversion–introversion. II is *anxiety*. III is called *cortertia*, since in the O-A battery it goes with measures of cortical alertness. IV is *independence*. VII is *intelligence* as a broad second-order factor. VIII has been called restraint, *control*, or good upbringing, because it combines higher superego with desurgency (prudence) and a well established self-concept, Q_3.

There are two theories about secondaries: (1) that, like primaries, they are due to some single cause affecting all of the primary set, and (2) that they are "emergents" due to mutual interactions of the primaries with a normal environment. If we consider the first two secondaries in the preceding paragraph in the light of these theories, we may explain the exvia–invia pattern, as Jung did, as some common, largely constitutional, contribution to each of the four factors A, F, H, and Q_2. Alternatively, we can suppose that a person

TABLE 6.1. Second-Order Change Structures on a Broader Basis of Normal and Pathological Primaries

	I	II	III	VI	VIII	Depression	Psychoticism	(9)
A	54		− 32					
C		− 55		32				
E	57			36	(08)	28		− 59
F	95			06	(− 09)			
G	24				69			
H	49	(− 02)	− 47	29	− 23			− 28
I		− 72						
L		(− 03)		62	− 33			
M			− 44	(− 15)				
O	34	38	− 33					
Q_1				86	− 27			
Q_2	− 40		− 37	41				− 38
Q_3	− 44	− 54			62			
Q_4		96						
D_1	21					55		
D_2				29		55		− 28
D_3				− 37	− 28	35		− 25
D_4				− 49		54		59
D_5		23				51		
D_6	32	30				54		
D_7						83		
Pa		36					66	
Pp	− 20			− 32			(10)	− 59
Sc			27				61	
Ag				− 35			45	
Ps							74	

Note: Decimal points omitted as in all factor-loading tables. Intelligence *B* and shrewdness *N* have been omitted as variables since they define no factor. Second-order factors V, VI, and VII are not recorded; two are not present and VI has no loading of the pathological factor except 0.32 on *Pp* psychopathic. The label "untamedness" given a VI is fully supported by this new association. The anxiety factor has only a trivial association with depression items, (the factors, however, correlate 0.3); superego loads anxious depression; except for D_3 brooding discontent the depression primaries all load roughly to an equal degree on the general depression factor. The existence of the general psychosis state — loading highest on the general psychosis primary *Ps* and omitting the psychopathic primary — is a new discovery. *Source*: From *Personality and Mood by Questionnaire* (Cattell, 1973b). Reprinted by permission.

initially gifted in one of these traits tends to provoke, by environmental experience, the others. For example, a natural self-sufficiency, Q_2, may clog up a person's warmth, A, and give him little
exercise in surgery, F.

Similarly, two theories can be held to explain the rise of the second factor, trait II, anxiety. First, we may suppose that a weak
genetic contribution to ego strength has permitted frustrations, Q_4,
to accumulate, and that the transformation to anxiety is accentuated
by low H and high guilt proneness, O, with a poorly developed self-
sentiment ensuing. This would be the Freudian picture of anxiety,
emanating from frustrations and a weak ego. Alternatively, we can
suppose that a single cause, presumably genetic and fitting the high
genetic determination found for anxiety, has appeared in a high
physiological anxiety proneness, and that this has undermined C
and Q_3, and encouraged O, low self-esteem.

Whichever explanation one favors, it is valuable in therapy to
obtain scores on anxiety, invia, and other secondaries because their
roles in mental health and adjustment are well known. We obtain
these scores from a weighted sum of the primaries (slightly different
from the weights above) given in the Handbooks. In the case of the
O-A battery the scores are obtained directly, because the primaries
in objective tests correspond to second orders in questionnaires. The
clarity of separation of neurotics by the O-A battery is shown in
Figure 6.3.

There can be little doubt, e.g., from the recent work on the Ger-
man O-A by Schmidt and Häcker, that measuring the second-order
factors by the O–A gives better diagnosis than any questionnaires.
However, 4 to 5 hours of testing, in place of 1 hour on the CAQ,
is more than many busy clinicians can tolerate. Resistance to the
O-A, however, has been based more on misunderstanding of its
scientific foundations than on time demand. To clarify the *former*,
we set out in Table 6.2 a typical piece of evidence on the factor structure of the O-A factors. It will be seen therein that (a) they load
on the markers (two) commonly set out for each, and (b) load the
questionnaire primaries in the appropriate second-order factor patterns for QVII (*U.I.* 17), QIV (*U.I.* 19), QI (*U.I.* 32), and QII
(*U.I.* 24) (Cattell and Birkett, 1980b). It also supports our later

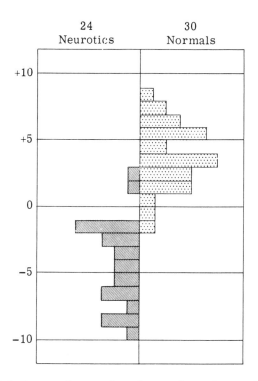

FIGURE 6.3 Extent of separation of neurotics and normals by the O–A battery (vertical axis-score on the O–A composite). From *The Meaning and Measurement of Neuroticism and Anxiety*, by R. B. Cattell and J. H. Scheier. New York: Ronald Press, 1961. © 1961 Ronald Press. Reprinted by permission.

argument (p. 84) that what we there call (and define) as the *five panels of ego action* do in fact load on the control factor, U.I. 17, and on an ego strength versus anxiety factor, *U.I.* 24.

In any case, the practice of *depth psychometry* — the simultaneous use of primary and secondary scores, is valuable. Two people may score equally high on a single anxiety scale, but actually do so through a very different combination of scores on the primary components *C*, *H*, *L*, *O*, Q_3, and Q_4. To the alert psychotherapist, much is signaled by such differences. For example, a person who is very low on *C* factor (ego strength) needs a very different treat-

TABLE 6.2 Illustration of Alignment of Second-Order Questionnaire and First-Order O-A Factors[a]

Variables	Assertion U.I. 16	Control QVII U.I. 17	Independence QIV U.I. 19	Evasiveness U.I. 20	Mobilization U.I. 23	Reality contact U.I. 25	Exvia vs invia QI U.I. 32	Anxiety QII U.I. 24
1. U.I. 16 O-A battery marker 1	0.80	-0.34	0.46	0.07	-0.02	-0.00	0.01	0.01
2. U.I. 16 O-A battery marker 2	0.81	-0.15	-0.02	-0.59	-0.06	-0.03	0.06	0.04
3. U.I. 17 O-A battery marker 1	-0.09	0.70	0.06	-0.03	-0.01	0.09	-0.09	-0.21
4. U.I. 17 O-A battery marker 2	-0.50	0.66	0.09	-0.01	-0.02	0.21	-0.02	0.07
5. U.I. 19 O-A battery marker 1	-0.02	0.20	0.22	0.08	-0.02	0.08	-0.16	0.10
6. U.I. 19 O-A battery marker 2	0.09	0.01	0.36	-0.09	0.08	0.11	0.12	-0.05
7. U.I. 20 O-A battery marker 1	-0.09	-0.08	0.02	0.48	-0.02	0.00	0.06	0.04
8. U.I. 20 O-A battery marker 2	0.13	0.25	-0.30	-0.00	-0.00	0.09	0.14	0.08
9. U.I. 23 O-A battery marker 1	-0.05	-0.17	-0.01	0.04	0.55	0.29	-0.09	-0.04
10. U.I. 23 O-A battery marker 2	0.03	0.06	0.56	-0.23	0.46	0.11	0.03	-0.20

11. U.I. 25 O-A battery marker 1	−0.20	0.36	0.16	0.07	−0.06	0.50	−0.04	−0.11
12. U.I. 25 O-A battery marker 2	−0.28	0.22	0.22	0.02	−0.02	0.40	0.10	0.12
13. Ego strength questionnaire. Panel 1	−0.00	0.46	0.07	−0.04	−0.04	0.03	0.06	−0.39
14. Ego strength questionnaire. Panel 2	−0.03	0.18	0.28	0.15	0.02	0.06	0.03	−0.43
15. Ego strength questionnaire. Panel 3	−0.18	0.29	−0.07	0.04	−0.06	−0.06	−0.09	−0.46
16. Ego strength questionnaire. Panel 4	0.07	0.53	−0.07	−0.05	−0.02	0.07	−0.14	−0.54
17. Interpersonal relations questionnaire	0.07	−0.01	0.08	−0.05	0.14	0.01	0.13	−0.29
18. Parental training relations	0.10	0.26	0.28	0.34	0.11	−0.02	0.19	−0.24
19. High impulse control in frustration	−0.00	0.10	0.04	−0.13	0.01	−0.28	−0.07	−0.64
20. Ego strength. 16 PF C. Form B	−0.04	−0.19	0.22	−0.02	−0.03	−0.01	0.06	−0.58
49. 16 PF A primary. Affectia	0.06	−0.32	−0.05	−0.10	−0.01	−0.04	0.63	−0.15
50. 16 PF B primary. Intelligence	0.05	0.22	0.13	−0.00	0.01	−0.07	−0.05	0.07
51. 16 PF C primary. Ego strength	−0.00	0.08	−0.01	0.02	−0.05	0.18	−0.04	−0.93

(continued)

TABLE 6.2 (Continued)

Variables	Assertion U.I. 16	Control QVII U.I. 17	Independence QIV U.I. 19	Evasiveness U.I. 20	Mobilization U.I. 23	Reality contact U.I. 25	Exvia vs invia QI U.I. 32	Anxiety QII U.I. 24
52. 16 PF E primary. Dominance	-0.07	-0.33	0.23	0.11	-0.03	0.07	0.55	0.08
53. 16 PF F primary. Surgency	0.21	-1.00	0.01	0.06	0.07	0.03	0.62	0.06
54. 16 PF G primary. Superego	-0.02	1.05	-0.04	0.18	-0.02	0.01	0.01	-0.06
55. 16 PF H primary. Parmia	0.13	-0.58	0.00	0.05	-0.09	0.08	0.68	-0.31
56. 16 PF I primary. Premsia	0.03	-0.00	-0.42	-0.10	0.08	0.11	0.09	0.00
57. 16 PF L primary. Protension	-0.00	0.06	0.21	-0.01	0.02	0.04	0.43	0.14
58. 16 PF M primary. Autia	0.05	-0.09	0.17	-0.12	-0.55	0.01	0.18	-0.01
59. 16 PF N primary. Shrewdness	-0.09	0.35	-0.01	0.00	-0.09	0.16	-0.09	0.27
60. 16 PF O primary. Guilt proneness	0.13	0.27	-0.18	-0.18	-0.06	0.02	-0.17	0.48
61. 16 PF Q_1 primary. Radicalism	0.01	0.15	0.27	-0.09	-0.26	0.03	-0.06	-0.12
62. 16 PF Q_2 primary. Self-sufficiency	0.01	0.20	0.01	-0.07	-0.08	0.05	-0.80	-0.01
63. 16 PF Q_3 primary. Self-sentiment	0.04	1.03	0.03	-0.03	-0.05	0.02	-0.07	-0.26
64. 16 PF Q_4 primary. Ergic tension	0.04	0.08	-0.05	-0.06	0.16	-0.03	0.10	0.76

[a]This is an excerpt from a larger table (Cattell and Birkett, 1980), with many variables added to fix the hyperplane simple structure.

ment from one whose anxiety springs more from a high frustration (Q_4) and perhaps an undeveloped self-sentiment (Q_3). Depth psychometry compares the primary test result profile *simultaneously* with the secondary scores (using weights given in the *Handbook*). Exvia, anxiety, cortertia, independence, and control all have appreciable predictive weights on clinical criteria. The further psychometry of *statistically* combining primary and secondary scores is discussed elsewhere (Cattell, 1973b; Cattell and Johnson, 1984).

Secondary structure in the *motivation* domain is still in need of further clarification, because it involves factoring ipsative scores, but the careful work of Boyle (1984) shows that traumatic stressful stimuli cause fear and superego to increase and mating and narcism to go down significantly. Regression, stress, anxiety, and depression (see Table 6.3) form one second-order factor among the general states, and arousal and low fatigue and probably exvia form a second distinct factor (Cattell, 1973b). It is a noteworthy finding that the personality primaries in the CAQ, the motivation-dynamic factors on the MAT, and the state factors on the 85 Q prove to be essentially in different spaces, except for a few instances commented upon already.

Practically, this has the advantage of generating high predictions (multiple R's) when we go to the trouble of including nondynamic traits (16 PF, CAQ), dynamic traits (MAT), and passing states (85Q) in measurements of one and the same individual (Boyle, 1983). These present results do not fit the notion of a single source of energy behind all the ergs, but until further work we would accept that possible conclusion on other grounds. Although the CAQ, the MAT, and the 8-State Questionnaire are thus proven each to bring new information not covered by the others, there is an exception in the case of two traits, the self-sentiment and the superego, which are the same traits (in CAQ and MAT) measured respectively by questionnaire and by objective tests. These may be assessed by either test, but preferably, to reduce instrument factor effects, as a mean of both.

As to higher strata structure in the general states, the evidence is rather conclusive, as stated above, that three second orders subtend the primaries in the Cattell–Curran 8-state battery, as shown

TABLE 6.3 The Structure of Higher-Order Psychological State Dimensions

(1) Factored on a Single Occasion[a]

Variables	α	β	γ
Exvia	− 26	−67	16
Anxiety	89	14	00
Depression	61	45	05
Arousal	− 15	−77	− 06
Fatigue	28	68	− 01
Stress	71	12	− 09
Regression	60	35	04
Guilt	83	01	08

(2) Factored as State Difference Scores
Third (second order) stratum of state Q-data dimension

		Curran dR-technique			
	Variables	α	β	γ	δ
I	Exvia	−66	− 04	− 12	47
II	Anxiety	87	− 02	− 03	07
III	Depression	09	−82	26	− 13
IV	Arousal	− 10	− 35	08	84
V	Fatigue	42	54	11	− 08
VI	Stress	06	12	73	− 07
VII	Regression	− 05	− 04	46	− 56
VIII	Guilt	− 08	− 47	− 19	− 15

	Barton P-technique			Boyle dR-technique		
Variables	α	β	γ	α	β	γ
Exvia	−41	− 03	− 01	00	− 02	− 09
Anxiety	79	02	04	94	− 17	− 07
Depression	− 04	−75	− 10	61	19	−17
Arousal	− 08	−53	− 07	− 27	− 39	16
Fatigue	04	35	01	− 01	89	− 04
Stress	03	08	09	55	17	10
Regression	− 02	− 02	42	56	13	−14
Random	36	− 01	41			
Guilt				68	− 04	04

Note: Decimal points omitted as in all factor-loading tables.

[a]This is from G. Boyle's (1985) factoring along with the MAT, in which β corresponds to super ego in MAT. It has been hypothesized (Cattell, 1973b) that the single-occasion state measures combine states with underlying traits. The result, in this and other analyses, is two major factors: one with anxiety, depression, stress, regression and guilt, and some invia, and the other with low arousal, fatigue, invia, and some depression. [See (1) above

in Table 6.3. These results are, however, from *R*- and not *dR* technique and may therefore represent underlying *trait* effect on states.

In this chapter we have examined the nature of the relations among traits and among states. We have seen also how a profile of source trait scores can be equivalent to an assignment to *types*. We have argued also why depth psychometry, *simultaneously* heeding primary and secondary scores, gives a broader view of structure and of development in a single clinical case.

It is always highly important to distinguish between traits and states. Testing with the Curran–Cattell 8-state battery, for example, shows (Cattell and Brennan, 1982; Boyle, 1984) that the states are highly susceptible to change of situation, as also are some U measures on the MAT. The modulation model development, added into the behavioral equation, is a precise and effective way of handling prediction from state measures along with traits. But insufficient work has yet been done by clinical psychologists to determine the *k* values of the common situations we need to use in practice. Nevertheless, as a mode of conceptual thinking, the modulation model is essential to clear clinical thinking and appraisal.

Incidentally, it is possible to continue factoring from the second- to a third-stratum analysis. Reasonably consistent results have been obtained in the questionnaires. But these we must presently leave to special research reading (Cattell, 1973b).

With this chapter we conclude the work of describing the patient and his changes in terms of (1) *primary general traits*, such as surgency, protension, and superego strength, (2) *secondary general traits*, such as anxiety, cortertia, and exvia–invia, (3) *primary dynamic traits*, such as ergic tensions and sem levels of development, (4) general *states*, such as regression, anxiety, and stress, and their secondary derivatives, and (5) *types*, as in the DSM.

---

in table.] In the pure states [(2) above in table], agreement, mutually, is not high, favoring the theory (Cattell, 1973b) that each involves change to a particular stimulus; e.g. Boyle's terrifying film, causing co-change in particular states. However, one sees a systematic difference from the trait-contaminated patterns in anxiety (α) containing less stress, regression, and depression, which must belong in (1) for trait reasons. Also the depression is a factor less tied to fatigue and low arousal, which we must suppose link through one of the primary personality factors, e.g., *O* factor.

Chapter 7

Decision, Conflict, and Integration in the Ego

Learning normally occurs when existing habits fail to achieve desired goals. This learning may be the result of a new external change causing frustration, where previously there had been adaptation. Before learning takes place there is, in humans, normally conscious consideration of the situation and a decision to try a new course of action. The outcome of the decision between one course of action, j_1, and another, j_2, will naturally depend on the relative strength generated in the two courses of action. These strengths we can express by the two behavioral equations, arising in the same situation, k, and in the face of the same or a slightly different stimulus. For example, a person may have to decide whether to play tennis or go for a swim when his host offers the alternative. This means two courses of action, j's, potentially generated by one situation and stimulus.

If we knew the weights—the b's (or v's or s's)—for the satisfactions to various drives, temperament traits, and abilities in these two activities, we could insert the person's trait strengths in the two behavioral equations and see which comes out stronger, thus:

$$a_{hij_1k} = b_{hj_1k_1} T_{1i} + b_{hj_1k_2} T_{2i} + \cdots + b_{hj_1kp} T_{pi} \qquad (7.1a)$$

$$a_{hij_2k} = b_{hj_2k_1} T_{1i} + b_{hj_2k_2} T_{2i} + \cdots + b_{hj_2kp} T_{pi} \qquad (7.1b)$$

The same antithesis can be expressed for two courses of therapeutic action. The response course of action a_{j_2} will be followed if a sum of the component terms is greater than for j_1. Now any such decision will probably be accompanied by some sense of overt, active conflict. An expression of the degree of that conflict will be greater the less the difference of the a's, i.e., the closer the decision, and presumably the greater their sum, the more important the issues. Thus we can express an estimate of the conflict that is involved most simply by c_a (a for "active") in the following:

$$c_a = \frac{a_{hij_2k} + a_{hij_1k}}{a_{hij_2k} - a_{hij_1k}} \tag{7.2}$$

Cattell & Sweney (1964) have taken a very different course to provide a possible check on this formula by providing a measure of the expressed conflict criterion, c_{ai} itself. They set out to factor the common array of *signs of conflict* and have shown the existence of five clinically meaningful factors. But so far no one has related these measures to that given by equation (7.2) — or some modification thereof, clinically and experimentally.

The five expressions of conflict factored out by Cattell and Sweney (1964) are:

1. *Cognitive disturbance in suppressive action.* Appearing in mistakes in cancellation performance, in motor performance, interference with attention, etc.

2. *Restriction of attention.* Appearing in reduced attention to conflict-provoking stimuli; rejection of humor on topic; little confidence in a confluent solution.

3. *Fantasy, from perplexity and frustration.* Appearing in fantasy of easy solutions, vacillation, suggestibility, many middle-category solutions.

4. *Advanced ego action.* Appearing in *enhanced* perception of conflict-evoking stimuli, little internal inconsistency of action preferences; greater confidence in existence of a confluent solution.

5. *Tension-impulsivity.* Appearing in muscle tension, changeabil-

ity, mistakes in immediate memory (in coding), more pugnacity
and more anxiety in contemplating solutions.

The last (at any rate as anxiety) is widely recognized as a sign
of conflict, but the others are also evident to the alert clinician. The
experimental results show that the above five manifestations apply regardless of the psychological locus of the conflict.

Through integrative learning (the third of the five principles
enunciated in Chapter 1), most conflict ends in some compromise
in which the individual accepts a new course of action, yielding
deprivation in some drives in return for greater satisfaction in others.
This leads to a third expression of conflict action, somewhat different from equations (7.1) or (7.2) above, and results usually in
a behavioral equation with some negative b's (to be precise, s's).[7]
We realize that these negatives represent the deprivations outbal-
anced by positives, as in the following example. From the equation we can pick out the negative b's, and sum them to a $\bar{b}^2$, while
the positive b's in the behavioral equation sum to $\overset{+}{b}{}^2$.

$$c_n = \frac{\Sigma \bar{b}^2}{\Sigma \overset{+}{b}{}^2 + \Sigma \bar{b}^2} \tag{7.3}$$

The squaring is to reach the variance contributed by each kind, and
to eliminate negative values. This is a fair statement of the *loss*,
through conflict, in the given course of action. (The denominator
gives the *total* ergic involvement of which this loss and *suppression*
is thus written as a fraction of the total involvement.) This *indurated*
conflict, c_n, thus represents the internal loss of satisfaction by "fric-
tion." Presumably when it reaches a point where the denominator
and numerator approach equality and $c_n = 1$, the person will aban-
don the course of action as containing no satisfactions. Meanwhile
research needs to compare c_n scores so calculated with the Cattell–
Sweney conflict factors and with the (U-I) conflict scores to give
us more understanding of the full relationships of these diverse con-
ceptions and values for conflict.

However, a major contribution to this understanding was made by J. R. Williams (1959), who argued that to determine a value for the *total* averaged ergic expressions lost by indurated conflict in a given person, one should obtain a measure of c_n over a *representative set* of the *total* life attitudes. He found the sum of c_n's to be significantly higher for a set of hospitalized patients than for normals. Unfortunately, in the thousands of psychological research articles since, not one has set out to report a check on this vital experiment. It certainly makes good sense, however, that individuals with genetic obstacles to adjustment or a superfluity of early "Freudian" traumatic experiences, would finish up with poorer, less rewarding, solutions in their indurated conflicts. Indeed it makes sense to derive an index of *goodness of integration* (of the total person's needs) as the *obverse* of c_n in equation (7.3) above, thus:

$$I_i = \frac{1}{C_m} \text{ [or alternatively, } (1 - xC_n)] \tag{7.4}$$

where I is the total integration and C is the sum of c's across the representative attitudes. There is evidence that C_n (or $1/C_n$) correlates significantly with factor C (ego strength) and also with total emotional *stability* (absence of score change) operationally measured on a representative set of attitudes, over an interval of a month or so (Cattell, 1943). Evidently we are centering in these dynamic c_n measures on a general personality trait of emotional stability — namely, on C factor, ego strength in the questionnaires. This equates the integration concept with ego strength.

Much evidence now indicates that ego strength (C factor), showing itself in questionnaire items as stability of purpose, absence of general emotional dissatisfaction with life, and capacity to give preference to long-term satisfaction over immediate impulse, is evidently one of the most important general personality factors, especially in clinical work. It therefore deserves special scrutiny at this point, particularly in clarifying its distinction from the factors found for the superego, G, and the self-sentiment, Q_3.

The superego fits the guidance given by moral concerns, as defined by Freud, and commonly accepted as conscience or superego. Q_3 is a factor unknown to clinicians before factor analysis, though the new evidence shows that, in guiding behavior, it is evidently *regard for the self-concept* and self-esteem in preserving social reputation. Since social reputation is in part moral, it is not surprising that we find *some* loading, *jointly* with *G*, on moral and religious values. But primarily it is a sentiment built around the self-image and concerned to maintain behavior in agreement with the self-image as socially learned and approved. Let us record the behavioral association of *C* factor, in ratings and in life criteria, beginning with Table 7.1.

In contrast to the self-sentiment, *C* seems to operate with little obvious imaginative, cognitive control from ideas themselves. It is simply a set of habits of reaction learned by trial and error to be more rewarding in the long run than the immediate responses to

TABLE 7.1 Known Relations of the Ego Strength Factor, *C*

Relation of *C* measures with ratings and behavior records
    Positively with: Emotional stability
                       Maturity
                       Readiness to face realities
                       (With *GZ* scales of activity, ascendance, objectivity, and "masculinity")

    Negatively with: Unstable
                       Easily annoyed
                       Dissatisfied with life
                       Sleep disturbances, etc.
Occupational associations
   Higher than average in administrators, group leaders, stress jobs (*not* mailmen, janitors, and "own pace" jobs)
   High in Olympic athletes, military cadets, research scientists, garage mechanics, electricians, airline pilots, nurses and hospital personnel, social workers, and police
   C factor correlates with occupational success: .37 as psychiatric technicians; .18 with drivers' freedom from accidents; .10 with salesmen's success; .30 with counselor effectiveness; .70 with football performance; .34 with teaching effectiveness, and positively with most achievement measures.

Clinical associations
   Exceptionally low in neurotics (especially anxiety neurotics), with substance abuse, homosexuality, criminality, manic depressive illness, schizophrenia, suicide, coronary disorders, sex and exhibitionist disorders
   No difference between men and women.

---

ergic impulses, which they replace. We can recognize the following five processes or "panels" in the action and growth of the ego.

   1. *Halting.* Calling a momentary inhibition to any strong impulse in order to examine the decision to be made. This may involve, in reverse, Burt's (1927) "innate general impulsiveness."
   2. *Inner evaluation.* A sensing of the real strength of the impulse and of others that may come into conflict with its end result. This can be a direct evaluation of trait strengths or aided by CET (*c*ue *e*vocation of *t*raits, discussed below).
   3. *Outer evaluation.* An examination of the external world situation. This involves consideration of past consequences of such actions as are indicated, with emotional realism and adequate retrieval of experience from the past.
   4. *Decision.* This involves a weighting of (1) and (2), not necessarily consciously, but nevertheless quantitatively. Thus, in the case of an undesirable, immoral act (a_{hijk}) we are likely to have

$$a_{hijk} = s_{hjk1} T_{1i} + s_{hjk2} T_{2i} - s_{hjkc} C_i - s_{hjkg} G_i - s_{hjkq} Q_3 \qquad (7.5)$$

Here we take just two traits (probably ergs, T_1 and T_2, back of the impulse) and assume the impulse is an antisocial one, filled with foreboding of future punishment. In this case the contraweight is not only of C but also of G and Q_3, which will be thrown into the scale against it (negative b's), and the action (a_{hijk}) will normally be brought to zero and rejected.
   5. *Effective implementation.* Equation (7.5) defines a dynamic decision and is therefore put in s's — indicators of satisfaction — rather than b's. The effectiveness with which the decision is maintained, however, will depend partly on the b's (and the addition of v's, expressing the traits' powers to act). In this action we must suppose that C reaches out to bring in the particular ergs and sems that will be its allies in the action against T_1 and T_2. It will do this by the cognitive action of *cue evocation of traits*, i.e., rallying the inactive traits by evoking the cognitive cues that it knows will arouse them to assist. Thus a man fighting a tendency to drink too much at the end of the day may well, as part of C action, recall his wife's distaste (a

weight on the wife sem) if he arrives home in an intoxicated condition and, by dwelling on this, overcome his drinking impulse.

The roles of the above panels have been shown factor analytically to be part of C (Cattell and Birkett, 1980b), as shown in Table 6.2. C has also been shown (Cattell, 1982) to have a 50 percent genetic variation among humans, and we can probably locate this in the action of the frontal lobes in producing the initial arrest of a strong impulse (panel 1).

The only weak point yet discovered in the above formulation of C is that C proves to have only a trivial correlation with intelligence, whereas we might expect that in the action of panel 3 intelligence would enter appreciably. The answer is probably that *blind* trial and error (means–end, law of effect) action still prevails in most life actions, the full consequences of reward or punishment of which are beyond our perception (result of panel 5). The ego is thus a reaction system built up by conditioning, from the relative rewards and punishments of distant and immediate consequences. It is, as Freud said, amoral in itself, simply seeking to maximize long-term satisfaction; therefore it is not surprising that some semblance of it exists in animal behavior, as Royce, Holmes, and Poley's factorings seem to show (1975).

In spite of all the forces and devices that the ego uses to maximize ultimate satisfaction and adaptations, it succeeds only to a limited degree. H. G. Wells has criticized the social assumption that a person is a single entity, saying that the individual's part systems and moods make him, socially, an undependable set of separate systems. This waywardness exists, and it explains why we all deplore neuroticism and admire ego strength in our companions. If we look at the dynamic lattice we realize that it is in a continual state of changing emphasis. The various ergic tensions alter basically in strength with physiological appetite, changing the reactivity of the subsidiated attitudes. At the same time the externally stimulated activation levels of sems combine with the ergic play to produce a living kaleidoscope of changing reactivities. It is surprising that the ego succeeds as often as it does in producing responsible, integrated action. In extreme cases the ego splits into two or more integrated systems in what clinicians encounter as *multiple personality*. But everyone has some degree of this instability, which involves shutting off certain memories necessary for control. Considering the time distance of reward from integrative action, it is not surprising that ego strength is usually far from its optimum development. On that scale a George Washington or a Lenin is an indispensable and treasured social entity.

This is the point in the discussion of the ego at which to recognize the action of what Anna Freud considered as the defense mechanisms. These are devices brought into action when the ego is likely to be overwhelmed by the strength of the opposition present in the impulse. They are essentially lies told in panel 4, bringing in other ergs and sems as allies. In *projection* there is a cognitive lie from "I hate him" to "He hates me," which no longer requires inner control by the ego. In *autism* the conflict is lessened by admitting fantasy satisfaction. In the defense mechanisms the call for direct action by the inadequate ego is avoided by *cognitive* rearrangements — but at the cost of ego growth. Theoretically, we might expect the stumbling upon an ad hoc defense mechanism to offer a temporary aid — a splint to hold the limb while it grows stronger. But, at least in clinically seen cases, the defense is likely to become permanent and stronger and become an obstacle to a more flexible action by a more mature ego. Certainly, as Cattell and Wenig (1952) show, particular personality factors seem to develop in connection with particular defenses, e.g., factor L with projection, factor M with fantasy, and so on. Until that research leads to development of a battery to measure defense mechanism styles, however, the mapping of these relations must remain speculative. Suffice it to say that defense measures, hastily undertaken when the ego is weak, tie up energies in an "ego substitute." This may account for our observation here that in most cases the "positive feedback" from ego successes does not lead to indefinite growth of the ego.

If we admit the not inconsiderable analogy between a group organization and the mind of an individual, we are compelled to recognize (Cattell, "On the Theory of Group Learning," 1953) — as shown in Barbara Tuchman's *The March of Folly* — that group learning is an extremely slow and "inefficient" procedure. But, by the realities of the analogy, we are compelled to recognize that normally the acquisition of ego strength is a far more complex and inefficient procedure than the individual's learning of a particular skill. The remoteness of rewards, the unpleasant stresses involved in control, and the changing dynamic foundation of the reward system soon bring a low efficiency of reward to "good" ego action. This fluidity has its group manifestations, which are the bane of the politician. The Russian Revolution of 1917 teetered on instability of loyalties among sems to the Tsar, the provisional government, the factory soviets, and the Bolshevik intellectual position — all of which went through many unpredictable changes, not to be expected in an electorate with more developed sems.

We cannot in this space pursue all the research evidence regarding the ego. C factor (the ego) remains the last, most complex mystery in psychology. The reader must be referred to ancillary reading (Cattell, 1980, pp. 375–414). But let us note that the genetic control (panel 1) is important (as witness also comparisons across species), and that the general factors of intelligence and memory, in panel 3, do not play as large a part as might be expected. This may be due to the fact that the more intelligent persons get into positions in which the demand on dangerous judgment actually increases. As Shakespeare said, "Checks and disasters grow in the veins of actions highest reared." In any case, if some form of toleration of frustration is part of ego growth, the less intelligent are more likely to have become inured by failure to that demand, thus putting a counter association on any tendency for C and $g_c(B)$ to become positively correlated.

It is true that of the age curves of trait development (Cattell, 1973b) that of ego strength most closely resembles crystallized intelligence, increasing rapidly in the young and then slowing down in middle life. These findings suggest an accumulation of experiential learning in both traits. Here again, however, we meet an apparent paradox. Every success (in trial and error) by the ego in gaining more future satisfaction increases the likelihood of the ego *again* succeeding. Yet we do not have a run-away positive feedback growth curve. This must be due to decreasing opportunities in the life-experience curve for greater gains. As Ecclesiastes reminds us, there is chance: the battle is not always to the strong, but "time and chance happeneth to them all." The ego deals with balancing outcomes in the future — and the future is always obscure and chancy. There is normally an approached limit to the gains from paying attention to the future. And the changeability of circumstances puts a limit to the gains of trial-and-error learning. Nevertheless, more research is needed on the normality of distribution of C scores, and on the growth of C in adult life.

The above five-panel analysis shows the psychotherapist where he can place his "teaching" emphasis in those attempts to strengthen the ego that arise in almost all clinical cases. It is clear that the ego has considerable cognitive content, so that, except for its constant "decisive" action, it might almost be thought of as being ability modality. First, in the above list of functions the individual needs cognitively to respect and call in whatever blocking capacity he has for inhibiting and considering impulses. Second, he needs to learn sensitivity to the real relative strengths of his desires. Third, he should learn to look at the social situation and bring in his superego and self-sentiment attitudes ("Is that the sort of thing I would do?"), which are commonly on the side of control. Finally, he needs to marshal his other general sentiments when they would operate in the decision against the expression of the undesirable influence. All but the first are learnable.

In connection with the last, let us note that *the level of development of sentiments* out of ergs — the I-U ratio measure — is itself a general aid to ego strength, as the use of the total I-U in the integration measure obtainable from the MAT shows. It means that the more there exist beaten conditioning paths for ergic expression in the sems, the less the ego has to cope with raw ergic expressions. The implementation in panel 5, by calling in sentiments favorable to control, is thus only part of the story of control. The general level of sentiment development in relation to ordinary life situations, but particularly of the master self-sentiment Q_3, is normally an adjunct to ego control. It might not be if the individual should change his life situation to a point where all his sems become inapt — but this is rare indeed.

In this chapter we have seen that the processes of decision, the outcome in conflict, the general level of indurated conflict suffered, and the action of the ego as an integrator can all be assembled in a quantifiable five-point model. The field has barely been researched by experimental clinical psychologists, but enough to show that the model is sufficiently correct to guide our reasoning on the treatment of individual patients.

It follows descriptively from the above and our later detailed account of the ripple action (p. 152) that the ego is continually changing in composition. We recognize this popularly in such statements as, "I was not myself when I made that decision." The situational stimuli and inner appetitive states of the moment are always introducing some bias. Thus we finish with a "wave theory" of the ego, in that it exists as a series of overlapping waves in a process of control. In this the inhibitions are called forth for different ergs at different times, and the overall goal suffers differences of emphasis.

NOTE

[7]The methodologically aware reader will recognize that a negative correlation between a trait and a course of action (a_{hijk}) can be interpreted in the usual three ways: (1) that increase in the trait causes a decrease in the action, (2) that an increase in the action reduces the trait, and (3) that some unknown third force simultaneously increases one and decreases the other. We favor the first two interpretations because of the general nature of the behavioral equation, and, of these, the second best fits common observation: that greater persistence in the course of action increasingly blocks the expression of the trait. Thus action and trait are in conflict when the correlation — b — is negative, involving a suppression of the trait (deprivation of satisfaction) in order to continue the action.

The reader will recognize that the correlational methods on which structured learning theory is based upon cut through the difference of "conscious" and "unconscious" determination. This is not to say that "cognition" — as known by the subject and argued for here as a means of therapeutic reconnection — has the determinism that current fashionable "cognitive theory" gives to it. Let us not forget that, as Fromm has recently (1973) reminded us, "Freud's discovery was that what we think is not necessarily identical with what we are, that what a person thinks of himself may be, and usually is, quite different from what he really is." This has the usual elliptical form of expression in clinical writings — how can thought be identical with the ego? — but it reminds us that recent cognitive psychology has forgotten some basics.

Chapter **8**

Involvement Indices Discovered by the Use of *P*-technique

We stand by the therapeutic model that both the b's (including s's) in the behavioral equation and the traits themselves can be altered to produce real learning changes. It has been illustrated, however, in actual cases in Chapter 4, that current psychology is rarely in possession of the b's for various symptoms, and that one therefore simply aims to shift the unknown b's and involvement indices in what one estimates from the loadings to be a desirable direction. The level of the T's is well estimated by our present structured tests, such as the CAQ and MAT, and we can verify, as we proceed, that we have moved traits in the desired directions (Cattell, 1975).

This one-handed approach can, however, be converted to a two-handed grasp if we use, diagnostically, what has been called *P*-technique — *factorization of the single person*. It has the advantage, also, that it yields the b values specific to that person, not a mere sample average, as in *R*-technique. However, the historical evidence that it has scarcely been used in the forty years since its introduction (Cattell, Cattell, and Rhymer, 1947) witnesses that it is too complex and demanding a method for use by the average clinician.

Nevertheless, we shall devote a brief chapter to it here, because, like the Wright Brothers' airplane, attention may improve its practicability, and because, in any case, it illuminates some points in the use of b's in structured learning theory.

The basic theory behind P-technique is simple enough; namely, that if two behaviors in a person are simultaneously high on Monday, low on Wednesday, and high again on, say, Saturday, their simultaneous appearance justifies us in concluding that they spring from a common trait and stimulation source. This is a piece of common sense that every clinician uses, but in his usual rough way.

In P-technique we make *measured* observations of the symptom and of various drive manifestations, every day, for, say, 100 days; by correlating their ups and downs, we seek the sources of the symptom. To do this by plotting a diagram would be most direct, but 50 variables would produce a skein of lines confusing to the eye. So we intercorrelate all 50 variables and factor the matrix to a set of simple structure factors. Those factor contributions to the ups and downs of the variables are likely to be the underlying sources, in the individual and his environment, of the changes in the observed variables.

In practice, the problems arise in getting measures that can be repeated without too much practice (learning) intrusion and in retaining the subject for a sufficient number of occasions — say 100 — to provide a sound statistical basis for the correlations. The first problem is overcome by setting aside, if necessary, a practice "instrument factor" in the final calculations. The second — two or three hours of testing a day for 100 days — has defied the scientific zeal of all but a few investigators like Birkett, Cross, Curran, De Fries, Kline, Hurley, Rhymer, Shotwell, Colley, Nesselroade, and a few others. However, the findings have been remarkably consistent in showing the presence of the same ergs (sex, fear, curiosity, etc.) and the same sems (to self, career, hobby, etc.) as in the R-technique analyses. In fact, we finish up with the same behavioral equation — though with b's peculiar to the individual, namely:

$$a_{hijk} = b_{hjk1}E_{1i} + \cdots + b_{hjkn}E_{ni} + \cdots + b_{hjkm1}M_{1i} + \cdots + b_{hjkmp}M_{pi} \qquad (8.1)$$

where h is the focal stimulus, k is the ambient situation peculiar to each occasion, the n E's are ergic tensions, and the p M's are levels of sentiment development or activation. The actual E and M levels will, of course, vary with the *modulator* index for each occasion — the s_k hidden in b_k.

Incidentally, it is recognized that there is usually some delay in a causal action, so that the level of, say, drinking, on Saturday will manifest itself more in some performances on Sunday. Accordingly, a refinement is to use "staggered *P*-technique," in which, after their discovery and measurement, the correlations are reevaluated with one and two days delay of the variables on the factors to determine dependence more exactly. As McArdle (1985) shows, however, that gain from staggering is actually trivial.

Probably the most thorough *P*-technique clinical case yet reported is Birkett's (Birkett and Cattell, 1978) description of an alcoholic judge, who had not profited from five previous psychiatric treatments. He was measured on 100 occasions on the regular 10-factor MAT, extended by an erg of dependence-(appeal), theorized by some as important in alcoholism. The objective devices (I factor) used were fluency on consequences, word association, and projection; U-factor devices used were self-estimate, projection, and (by the analysis in this case) word association.

In addition to the dynamic measures on the MAT (plus appeal), a measure was taken, as criterion, of strength of desire to take a drink. Many of the correlations with this criterion were significant, as shown in Table 8.1.

When converted from correlations to beta weights, however, only three or four were significant. We have used in Figure 8.1 the device of changing relations found to path coefficients, offering a hypothetical causal explanation. (Note the partialing out changes the sign of the correlation of some contributors.)

This recognizes the significant eight of the eleven contributing traits, seeing ergic tension in sex, fear, superego, and pugnacity as the main contributors to the need to drink. Opposed to the rise of this need are the sem to the wife, the narcistic erg, and the self-sentiment — which restraining combination makes excellent sense in the circumstances.

Some additional causal correlations are built into Figure 8.1 from the observed correlations, e.g., the reductive effect of the self sem

**TABLE 8.1 Correlations of Ergs and Sems
with Alcohol Need in Client X by *P*-Technique**

	I	*U*	*U – I*
Fear erg	.26	.30	.29
Assertiveness erg	– .10	– .01	– .03
Pugnacity erg	.17	.13	.15
Superego sem	.21	.23	.23
Wife sem	– .42	– .47	– .46
Sex erg	.28	.29	.29
Narcistic erg	– .53	– .65	– .61
Self-sentiment sem	– .24	– .22	– .23
Career sem	03	.01	.07
Home sem	02	.14	.07
Appeal (dependency) erg	– .02	– .13	.03
Alcohol need	.96	.96	1.00

Source: H. Birkett and R. B. Cattell (1978). Diagnosis of the
dynamic roots of a clinical symptom by *P*-technique: A case
of episodic alcoholism. *Multivariate Experimental Clinical Research*
3(4), 181. Reprinted with permission.
     There is unusually high consistency of *U* and *I* correlations
[showing the greatest tie-up with sex and fear ergs (positive)
and narcistic erg and sem to wife (negative)]. The theory of
alcoholism as dependency or career-bound is not borne out
here.

upon pugnacity from frustration. It should be noted that any transla-
tion from observed correlations to a path coefficient diagram has
certain degrees of freedom of analysis. Figure 8.1 and others that
are at first possible from the coefficients, need to be tested further
for goodness of fit by the methods of *structural equations*.

However, a great deal is cleared up by the correlations shown.
We know that the therapeutic solution requires a buildup of the
sentiment to the wife and the self sem, and some way of utilizing
(stimulating) the narcistic erg to control the drinking need. There
are some curiosities and complications that require attention. Does
the negative correlation of the sex erg with the sem to the wife indicate that the individual is unable to express sex with his wife? And
what is the meaning of the strange positive correlation of superego
with drinking? Is drinking a release from a too active superego?

The subsequent therapeutic interviews agreed very well with the dynamic structure found in Figure 8.1. The sex drive showed increasing evidence of an anarchic role, due to exclusion from simple expression in a strict early upbringing. The narcistic need also shows, by a higher *U/I* ratio, that it encounters considerable frustration of expression. The CAQ, incidentally, showed, in general personality, a manic tendency, which was treated successfully by lithium.

Subsequent developments in therapy showed that this man on the bench was in the midst of a spiritual transformation. Therein

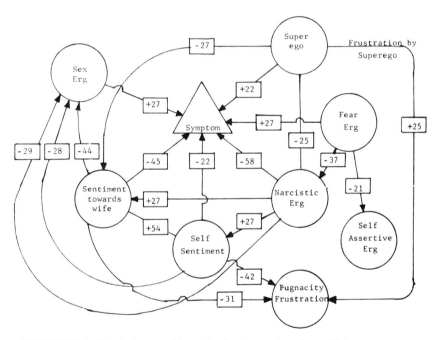

FIGURE 8.1 Deviations and hypothesized causal path coefficients among dynamic traits. The incircled square values are the first order correlations as arranged across nine *U* and *I* combination results. A negative sign is to be considered as inhibitive. From H. Birkett and R. B. Cattell (1978). Diagnosis of the dynamic roots of a clinical symptom by *P*-technique: A case of episodic alcoholism. *Multivariate Experimental Clinical Research, 3*(4), 173–194.

his narcism broke out in an evangelically prominent community service role, which later earned him the admiration of his community. Conceivably this fits the positive correlation between superego and drinking, in that he was seeking, in the latter, escape from the trammels of his humdrum court image. The correlation of both narcism and wife (negative) and sex (positive) with the drinking need itself actually increased in the course of therapy. It became evident that some new outlet of sublimation must be found for these drives, and eventually it was found in the new evangelical role, which he took on with complete cessation of alcoholism.

It has been suggested (Cattell and Birkett, 1980) that the demonstrated constancy of the dynamic analyses when made on 50 of the occasions — a statistically questionable number compared to the full 100 — indicates that a shortening of *P*-technique to a practically more acceptable period per patient may be possible. It is suggested also that the occasions could be contracted over perhaps a week (3 or 4 to each day) if a modus were introduced, e.g., a TV special movie, *to stir up a different gamut of emotions* on the different occasions. These improvements can only be decided upon by experiment, which is urgently needed if we are to bring to clinical psychology its *only* means of reaching objective and quantitative analysis of individual dynamics.

P-technique can be improved also by developing the objective measurement devices into shorter forms; by applying lead and lag correlations to factors relative to the data; and by applying the checks of structural equations to the hypothesized path coefficients that appear to fit the data.

Doubtless these developments will come — the forty years that the method has remained in pure science is no different from the forty years between Faraday and the first practicable dynamos. But for the present we set out the evidence without incorporating it further in the practical treatment discussed in this book.

Chapter 9

Representing and Evaluating the Situations of Learning

Without *P*-technique the therapist deals in his diagnostic CAQ, MAT, Anxiety, etc., profiles with *common* traits. He assesses the ergic tension level on, for example, the sex or fear erg, by means of a set of items common to humanity; these do not tell him anything about the *specific* life-situation investments or the history that brought about the observed ergic levels in an individual. This has to come through the interview. But at least he has already, from his instruments, an idea of where the stronger tensions lie and where sentiments (sems) are weak or strong. One must remember, however, that dynamic traits alter more, with adaptation and situations, than do ability or personality (style) scores. For example, in 3 testings on a young man at 2-year intervals, the sweetheart sentiment went from 5 to 10 and back to 5; the superego sentiment from 4 to 1 (in a destructive environment), and the sem to the parental home from a conflict-ridden 3 to a normal 5 (under accompanying psychotherapeutic examination of his attitudes to parents). These are relatively large changes, compared to those general in the population, but changes are to be expected with the passing experience of months and years — and, of course, of therapy. In this dynamic field, unlike the ability field, it is the *changes* that are of greatest therapeutic interest.

That therapy changes personality is taken for granted and cited in numerous clinical textbooks. Yet, as far as measured changes demonstrated in measured source traits are concerned, it is impossible to find experimental evidence.

In studying the origins and the backtrackings needed in therapy, it helps to think in terms of the model of the Adjustment Process Analysis (APA) chart shown in Figure 9.1.

This recounts the possible history of *any* drive that is stimulated to demand its satisfaction, and it enables us to "place" the problem of a given patient clearly, e.g., as D_2, E_1, F_3, and so on, according to the *choice point* at which the problem is presently arrested. This will help one to see what possible changes lie ahead, through what stages the patient has passed, and if steps need to be therapeutically retraced.

Another diagram that helps greatly in therapy is the dynamic lattice, as shown in Figure 9.2. This reminds us that all new behaviors are learned as "subsidiations" (to use Murray's term) to preexisting goals and, ultimately, to ergic goals. These ultimate subsidiations correspond to the loadings we find (ergs and sems) in the behavioral equation, when we factor analyze a cross-section of attitudes [equation (7.5)]. A large b before a particular erg (generally connoting a large s) in the equation tells us that the particular attitude course of action leads largely to the given erg. Naturally, most civilized, "integrated" behavior tends to lead through several sentiments (intermediate goals) to several ergic goals. On the left of this figure is a random set of a person's life attitudes. On the right are the ergs to which they ultimately subsidiate, and from which they draw their motivation. In between are a number of collections of attitudes around intermediate learned goals, which we call *sems*.

It is this dynamic lattice that the dynamically oriented clinician is called upon to unravel. He may use, instead of a factor analysis, the methods of free association, hypnotism, etc., used by Freud, but with reduced certainty. The connections in the lattice are both conscious — to be obtained by asking "Why do you do this?" — and unconscious (unknown to the patient), thus needing to be obtained by other methods. The correlational methods reveal the unconscious as readily as the conscious organic connections.

A third method of tracing connections — that of manipulative "blocking" — depends on the fact that if you block one path to the

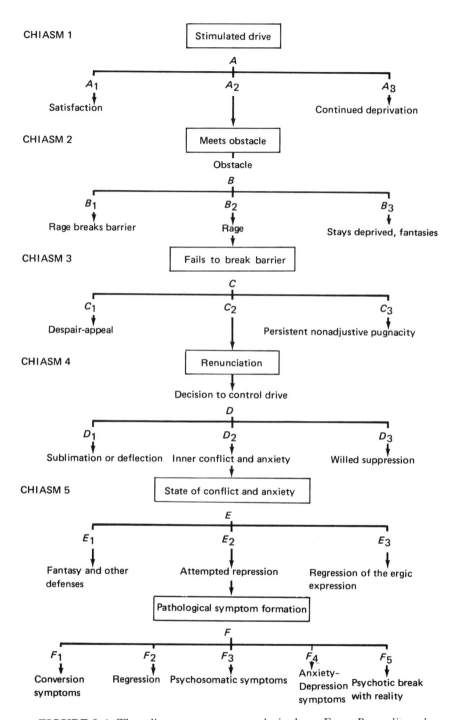

FIGURE 9.1 The adjustment process analysis chart. From *Personality and Learning Theory*, Vol. 2 (p. 307), by R. B. Cattell, 1980. © 1980 Springer Publishing Company, New York.

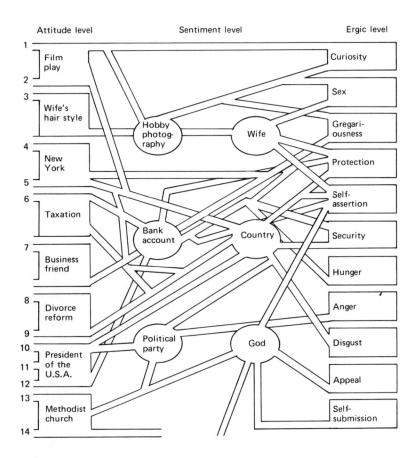

FIGURE 9.2 Fragment of a dynamic lattice showing attitude subsidiation, sentiment structure, and ergic goals. From *Personality and Learning Theory*, Vol. 2 (p. 77), by R. B. Cattell, 1980. © 1980 Springer Publishing Company, New York.

ergic or semic goal, some alternative paths will be strengthened. And, conversely, the easing of one path will detract from the use of the alternative others (Cattell, H., 1986). This need not be done physically: it will suffice to do it cognitively, in the imagination. For example, "If your mother were to die, what would you do about your career?" (not in Figure 9.2). The nature of the alternatives suggested will help indicate the ergic quality of the existing attachment. The converse, "If you had a big promotion in your job, what would you do?" is not so easy to trace, because the corresponding *withdrawals* of dynamic investments, e.g. from moonlighting jobs, might be slight and call for exploration over a larger area.

By whatever method — correlation, free association, or blocking — is used, the therapist does well to sketch, literally and in some detail, that part of the patient's dynamic lattice that includes the problem. Only then can he see the full range of options that are open to discussion and modification. We shall return to this in more detail when we consider methods of therapy in Chapters 10 and 11.

When the therapist needs to modify a trait he may, perhaps in half of all cases, seek to operate primarily by putting the patient in some new environmental situation. At present there is not nearly enough information in practitioners' handbooks, even in behaviorist handbooks, about what modifications are to be expected from various life situations. But we can proceed on the assumption that research will make it increasingly available (see Barton and Cattell, 1972, 1975). Meanwhile, a therapist may treat, say, a case of excessive shyness, in, say, a factory worker who always eats in the cafeteria alone, by arranging that she talk with people in the cafeteria line, and make plans to eat with one or two companions.

The origin of the level on any trait is the product of many experiences besides heredity. Since the number and value of these is greater than the practitioner could keep in mind or calculate from reliably, we have to turn, in any precise work, to matrices and matrix algebra, a device to calculate simultaneously from several variables. In life, in addition to quite personally peculiar paths of experience, we can recognize many paths that are essentially *common*, such as going to school, having to look after a younger sibling, trying one's success in a job, getting married, suffering a long illness, and so on. For each of these paths experienced by the person, we could obtain the average change produced in the principal CAQ, MAT, etc., traits; numbers for these expected magnitudes of change could be written down, across all traits, as a *vector* quantity, for the given learning experience. Then, if we want to estimate the change in a person who has *twice* as much experience of these paths as the average, we can write the resulting change in four or five traits, A, B, C, etc., as shown in Figure 9.3.

This may seem a relatively rough handling of the problem, for extensive repetition of an experience may increase the effect by, say, 1.4 instead of 2.0. But this is easy to arrange in the matrix. One may also wonder how best to obtain the values for the result of a single unit of experience of the path, used on the left of the equation (in Fig. 9.4), L, as the basis of calculation. The answer is that one can obtain the most stable values by measuring changes simultaneously for several paths, several traits, and several people, rather than by averaging for all people who take the path. In any case, research on situations in paths has to recognize that in life we can only very rarely measure changes due to a single situation and path; most of us are, willy-nilly, exposed to transit on a whole set of them, and are simultaneously following several paths in life. Then, according to the rules of matrix multiplication regime, we put the facts out as in Figure 9.4.

The first matrix, L, on the left is the *learning law* matrix, setting out paths α in equation (7.5) above for several traits, A, B, . . . Q_4, over *several* paths, α_1, α_2, etc., instead of one. The second, E, is the experience matrix, saying how frequently or to what degree each path has been transversed by each of the n persons, p_1 to p_n. The result of the multiplication is matrix T, which gives the resulting change for each person on each trait. The values are reached by the usual matrix rule of multiplying each row in L by each column in E, square for square, and adding up the products to a single value, on T, representing the total effect of all paths.

From this matrix equation, if we know *two* of the unknown matrices, we can calculate the third. In the classical situation, the therapist would be likely to know L (from a reference book) and E (from questioning his patients on their lives or from the courses

	Traits							Traits						
	A	B	C	D	E			A	B	C	D	E	Vector
Change from one experience of path α							Change from doubling experience of path α							multiplier
	.5	.2	.1	0	.3			1.0	.4	.2	0	.6	

FIGURE 9.3 Vector multiplier of traits for path experience.

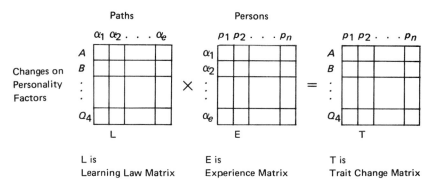

FIGURE 9.4 Path learning analysis (PLA) for trait vector changes, by matrix methods. α_1, α_2, . . . α_e represent, in L, path potency vectors, regarding path effects on traits. In E the α's as rows represent the frequencies (and/or intensities) with which people are exposed to the paths. From *Personality and Learning Theory*, Vol. 2 (p. 296) by R. B. Cattell, 1980. © 1980 Springer Publishing Company, New York.

of treatment behavior he prescribes). From these, he would calculate T, the expected trait changes. (In research, on the other hand, in which one sets out to *find L* values, one would work out T from measurements, and, knowing E, and working in reverse, *obtain* the learning law matrix L, to insert in the textbook.) When one knows the L matrix, the second matrix can, incidentally, be a *single* vertical vector for the single individual case concerned.

At present, except for a few situations studied by Barton and Cattell (1972, 1975), the therapist will have to *estimate* the L matrix himself, keeping to standard scores and his personal experience. The path learning analysis (PLA) matrix operation in Figure 9.4 can be carried to further designs, as may be read elsewhere (Cattell, 1980, p. 309), notably advancing to *determer potency analysis* (DPA), in which weight is given to size of *common "teaching" elements* that may occur in *any* path. In the end, as a part of personality learning theory, these analyses of the *gross* effect of experience on a trait need to be broken down into the actions of the five structured learning theory principles (cf. Chapter 1) used in DPA; but in practice the total effect in PLA L suffices.

Finally, in structured learning theory we need to recognize that each structural part of the dynamic lattice is not only a statement regarding active subsidiations, but also a complex statement of how behavior *actually unfolds itself* in a temporal process. It replaces the reflexologists' "chain reflex," which has failed to account for the "persistence toward a goal with varied responses" that is the essence of purposeful behavior. In Figure 9.5 the essence is laid out in the upper section.

It supposes that a drive, subscribed by $k_0 h_1$ starts out with the force $a_{k_0 h_1}$, which is aimed at subgoal SG_3. Reaching SG_1, the behavior does not continue automatically, but is reinforced by stimuli h_1 or h_2, according to which is encountered in greater strength, urging to proceed to subgoals $SG_{2(1)}$ or $SG_{2(2)}$, respectively. Which is chosen will depend on the relative present strength of h_1 and h_2. At these goals new situational stimulation occurs, at k_2, which, however, happens to be the same as $SG_{2(1)}$ and $SG_{2(2)}$ and propels the behavior to the subgoal SG_3. The original drive thus receives stimulation according to what turns up in the situation, and to which it reacts appropriately. But these s values, from previous experience at the h's, are such as to lead to SG_3 no matter what the k's at SG_1 direct. Only if a new situation, $k_{2(2)} h_3$, turns up, in the event of moving to $SG_{2(2)}$, which deflects into the new dynamic system of SG_6, will there be a change in the very purpose and goal.

Actual behavior is thus under a combined direction of drive, strength, E, regulated and represented by k's, and *stimuli*, h's, which may occur in varying strengths depending on the environment but for which behaviors equally likely to lead to the original goal (Figure 9.5) have been learned before. It will be seen that the tract in Figure 9.5 can be considered an enlarged part of the dynamic lattice, with the h's and k's inserted, which determines the *usual* direction of the behavior toward the ergic goal.

Although understanding the substance of this chapter — notably the nature of the dynamic lattice and the matrix evaluations in PLA and DPA — is more complex than learning the ideas in some other chapters, it deals with a *true* statement of the complexities and calculations with which a fully equipped therapist has to deal.[8] However, the absence from textbooks and handbooks of known numbers representing various life situations means that the psychometric

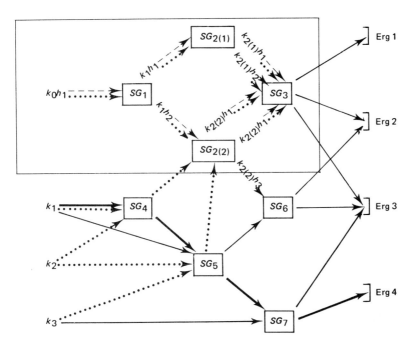

FIGURE 9.5 A sem as directing a process. Three kinds of abstractions are illustrated in this dynamic lattice. (1) A simple tandem *chain* from k_1 to Erg 4, by the heavy arrow. (2) A *sentiment* structure with the goal, subgoal SG_3, running from k_0, k_1, k_2, and k_3 the courses in which are shown by dotted arrows. (3) A *tract* beginning at k_0 and ending at SG_3, shown by dashed arrows. The remaining courses, e.g., those ending in the four ergs, are in simple lines. The sequences are shown in detail only in the tract. The subgoals are there numbered in order 1, 2, and 3, and the ambient situation k created by each is similarly numbered. At ambient situations k_1 and k_2 there are in each case two stimuli, h_1 and h_2, one of which will be paramount on any one occasion. From *Personality and Learning Theory*, Vol. 2 (p. 325) by R. B. Cattell, 1980. © 1980 Springer Publishing Company, New York.

equations often cannot yet be applied. Nevertheless, they are set out above in abstractions in order to both guide research in therapy and, at least, to clarify the conceptual procedures of the therapist.

Let us next consider in more detail the fact that the learning of a particular path calls for each trait to acquire a new, different b weighting.

It is evident that one source of changes, in both b's and T's, consists in changing the b attachments of any trait. An increase usually occurs in the weight b (generally depending on an increase in s) by showing that reward to a certain course of action will follow. This increase in reward can be achieved by conditioning — in behavior therapy — or simply by cognitive, insightful perception, gained through the consulting interaction, that such satisfaction is possible. In the latter case we are utilizing the "inner reward," which is intelligible only to structured learning theory and its understanding of the operation of sem structures. Another way is to inaugurate the *new behavior* by force of the ego, following appeal by the therapist, and let the patient discover that satisfaction follows from this direction. This change will become evident in the obtained b weights, but will be largely due to the change in v, and specifically in s, contained in the b's.

An example of the first would be to take a shy child, unable to speak in a group, and give him chances to speak where his knowledge is so much greater than the group's that each time he does so he is less aware of shyness. The changing s value this induced should spread to other group situations.

NOTE

[8]The concepts of structured learning theory are naturally difficult to assimilate by those trained only in classical reflexology. They turn the world from a simple, "penny-in-the-slot" action to a complex determining action of many personality traits, drives, and life situations. No scholarly survey of results of "behavioral theory" practice is given here, because such results are obvious repetitions of a partially workable but inadequate theory. They are well known, pragmatically, and would merely take the

reader here on a wrong, abortive course of thought. We take that whole "behavior therapy" reflexology (reflex arc) as read, and we embody the findings as oblique, partial aspects of structured learning developed here. As an S-R model, reflexology leaves out the powerful and complex action of O in the S-O-R model. Critics may say that journals are bulging with reflexological findings (monotonously repeated), whereas structured learning has perhaps a few dozen experiments only on which to base what they are pleased to call "mere unsupported theory." However, the few experimental supports are at the vital theoretical points, and the equations deal with measurable traits, ergs, sems, and situations, open to anyone to use. The statement that the structured learning theory equations are merely mathematical models is a lie, like the early chemical criticisms of the laws of Lavoisier, Dalton, Priestly, and others, made confidently by conservative alchemists. There is no need here to go further into the reflexological laws than their incorporation on the five principles in Chapter 1, since they are "known" by every undergraduate student.

Chapter **10**

Some First Principles in Structured Learning Therapy Practice

Thus far we have dealt more with diagnosis than with therapy — with the behavioral equation, the meaning of source traits, the evaluation of areas of conflict, the nature of the dynamic lattice, and the representation of situations in learning behavior. We now turn from the general theory of learning to the more particular problems of therapy — "How do you get someone to change his mind and alter his personality?"

It is generally agreed that psychoanalysis has achieved some success in shifting the b's and T's, and "behaviorism" i.e., reflexology) has certainly changed the b's for many specific behaviors, while varying success has been achieved by a host of special schools — transactional analysis, Rogerian methods, group therapy, psychoanalysis, regression therapy, dianetics, cognitive therapy, problem-solving therapy, enhancing self-esteem, and so on. Structured learning theory accepts that there are elements of truth and efficacy in these existing systems, but it goes beyond them in its formulation, in its practice, and, especially, in the precision of its model.

At this point, let us note that although we have spoken of producing changes in the b's — involvement of traits — and in the T's as separate aims, the factor analyst will recognize that they must be interrelated. The meaning and measurement of a trait depends on the behaviors marked by their pattern of high b's. If these alter, or a new behavior achieves a high b loading, the trait has altered in its expression and probably, therefore, in its score. For example, if a schoolboy's self-assertive erg shifts forward from the playing field to scholarly performance, the self-assertive erg must henceforth be measured by more weight on scores in the latter field. And although the factor trait structures show that, on average, higher dominance behavior is found in *both* business and home situations, a given individual may learn to show it less in one of these areas, so that the estimate of his level on the trait requires a different b weighting in that area.

It is evident, therefore, that one source of changes, in both b's and T's, consists in first changing the b attachments of any trait. An increase usually occurs in the weight b (generally depending on an increase in the contained s) through showing that greater reward will follow a certain course of action. This increase in reward can be achieved by conditioning — in behavior therapy — or simply by cognitively insightful perception, through the consulting interaction, showing the patient that such satisfaction is possible. In the latter case, we are utilizing the "inner reward," which is explicable only by structured learning theory; i.e., leading to understanding of the operation of sem structures that can be invoked. Another way is to inaugurate the new behavior by force of the client's ego decision, following appeal by the therapist, and let the patient discover that satisfaction ultimately follows from this initially logically "enforced" direction.

An example of the first would be to take a shy child, unable to speak in a group, and give him the opportunity to speak where his knowledge is so much greater than the group's that each time he does so he achieves an increase in his self-assertive erg and a deconditioning (extinction) of his fear response. An example of the second would be the insight given to a wife that she needs to smile and be warm on greeting her husband, in place of her unconscious lack of expression. An example of the third is to get a boy to join a sports team wherein, after a few experiences, he may find himself getting much more gregarious and achieving other satisfactions that he had not expected.

It should be noted that, insofar as the second-order factoring of ergs shows an erg to have a roughly constant total sum of energy in it, the encouragement of some ergic *b*'s will mean the reduction of others. The strategy of reducing an undesirable expression is partly, therefore, the encouragement and institution of *other* expressions. An alcoholic who continues to drink partly because he enjoys the company of his drinking companions may give up his habits more easily if he is introduced to new, nondrinking, congenial companions, as in Alcoholics Anonymous.

These intended adjustments are always easier and more efficient if the therapist works first to analyze and draw up the patient's main dynamic lattice diagram. This can be done by *P*-technique, or, without that labor, by the questioning and the free association that Freud used. From the drawn lattice it will be more readily seen which sentiments subsidiate to which ergs, and where fresh channels of satisfaction may successfully be sought. For example, in the fractional sketch of a lattice, in Figure 10.1, it will be seen that in this domestic problem a neglected wife has permitted herself a lover. Investigation shows that through the sem to the lover she obtains a companionship (gregarious erg) that her husband neglects to offer her. On the other hand, she is proud (self-assertiveness) of her husband's social position (self-assertion) and does not experience with him the fear to which consort with the lover exposes her. It would require little change in the husband's companionable behavior to more than overbalance the total ergic investment in the lover with that in the sem to the husband. In this case, a joint talk with husband and wife led the former to regret his neglect and to rebuild his wife's sentiment to him with its sex, gregarious, and self-assertive satisfactions, bringing an end to her unsatisfactory relation with the lover.

As Freud and Jung were the first to point out, the problem in most neuroses is unconscious complexes. By that we mean that certain connections in the lattice are unknown to the patient. There are two senses to the term *unconscious*. First, there is the sense just indicated, of a break in the conscious purpose of *why* one does an act, in the subsidiated steps in the lattice. This is common in symptoms, e.g., when a compulsive neurotic has an urge to count lamp

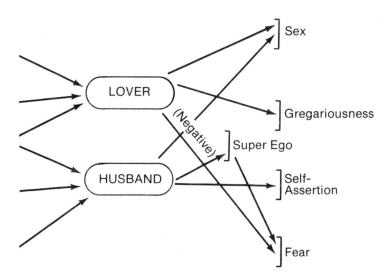

FIGURE 10.1 Uncovered fraction of a neurotic dynamic lattice.

posts on the street, not knowing why. Second, there is the cognitive inability to recall some name or place. The two may frequently be connected. Although Freud spoke of these as all or nothing phenomena, there is no doubt that they are matters of degree, shading into ordinary forgetfulness or partial unawareness.

Action rests on cognitively recognized (not necessarily consciously) stimuli. If we wish to prevent some action, the way to do it is to crowd out or suppress or repress a cognitive stimulus. A stimulus that is painful and tends to evoke some disturbing action is normally dismissed from the mind. The act of repression that does this is really the starvation of a memory, by focusing attention elsewhere. This is discussed in Jung's idea of "dis-association." That is to say, the engineering of an act of repression is not so much a positive act as the result of continually building up other associations, as Anna Freud recognized.

The lost association can sometimes be found through hypnotism, through analysis of dreams, through humor, or even through the tunes that a client is inclined to sing to himself—or simply through relaxed digging away at associations in the expected early life area, as in the practice of "regression therapy." When the association is found, it is commonly accompanied by a disturbing affect — that which led to its repression. Here we meet the question of *abreaction*. If, say, a person has an avoidance reaction to dogs, for no sound reason he can give, and an experience can be brought to mind when at 3 years of age he was attacked by a dog, is it necessary for recovery that he *relive* that experience with all the terror it inspired at the time? Opinions of therapists differ on this; but at least if he recalls the whole episode, and realizes how unneeded his reaction was (or is in its adult perspective) he can place the experience in proportion and rid himself of his excessive avoidance reaction.

The number of such distortions in engrams from the past in the adult mind is probably far greater than we commonly suppose. This persistence is due to the superior potency of memorizing in early years, as well as the poor perspective that characterizes early emotional experiences. An adult suffering from excessive dependence on a parent figure saw that parent person, at one year of age, as the whole world. If insecure circumstances at that young age thrust his dependence to the fore, later experience is unlikely to bring it into proportion in the normal way, and the individual remains "fixated."

If we accept the Freudian theory that an erg (at least the sex erg) goes through developmental stages, from narcism, through homosexual urges, to heterosexuality, then an early acute experience will, additionally, cause the person to retain the phase of *ergic quality* at the time the traumatic overexpression occurred. The majority of our adult opinions and attitudes derive partly from current reasoning and partly from the poor or distorted perspectives of early childhood experiences. A substantial part of therapy, therefore, consists in making conscious the reasons for feeling the way we do, and reintegrating the objects of attitudes in a more rational adult perspective. This involves desensitization, as presented, for example, by Lazarus (1966).

The shifting of attitudes takes place largely from the resources in the individual's existing sems, and partly from being placed in new external situations. That is why an analysis of the individual's existing resources, by the CAQ and MAT, is so important for well-planned therapy. If we know from the MAT that an alcoholic has a strong career sem, we can proceed differently than if that sem is initially negligible in the given patient. It is an important lesson of structured learning theory that *the existing dynamic structures are the fulcra on which the levers of change can be rested*. With evidence of a strong career sem, one can assess the consequences of alcoholism upon it, and then cognitively begin to draw upon sufficient resistance to the habit to bring the patient to a decision to face some arduous aspects of therapy. And similarly with what we find about what ergs are outstanding in a person. In this connection, let us note that successful behavior therapy — changing a habit — occurs mainly when the total personality of the patient has already agreed to reject the symptom (as Francis Bacon noted long ago). Then, and only then, will he face the extinction process or the unpleasant treatment by chemotherapy (noxious stimuli in drink). The battle has to be won before the behavior therapy conditioning can be accepted. Behavior therapy must therefore operate within an appreciation of the total personality and a realization of what sems can be brought to the alliance with the ego.

In addition to this criticism of behavioristic therapy from the standpoint of its blindness to dynamic structure we must add its ignoring of the inner conditioning which goes on in human thought processes. A child may be currently exposed to a dozen reconditioning sessions, but the possibility exists of a thousand taking place in his mind. This has been seized upon in the recent practice of altering imagery. Revival of basic interest in the potency of imagery is largely due to the experiments of Cartwright. To connect idea A with idea B, so that the patient experiences a thousand conditionings in thought is probably most powerful when the ideas are presented as images. Imagery has a more natural connection with emotion (by reason of its primitiveness) than do abstract ideas. It is only a short step from this perception to the supplying of tapes to remind the patient in daily sessions of the imagery connections needed, as has recently become "fashionable." The possibility of far greater frequency of conditioning than behavior therapy has recognized, in the human mind's operations, is certainly a practical improvement.

Thus, at a first contact with the application of structured learning theory, we find:

1. There is a need for a comprehensive diagnostic measurement of the total personality, especially in its motivational dynamic structure.

2. We need to recognize that the b's and the T's to some extent change together.

3. Undesirable behaviors can be reduced by deliberate reward to *other* outlets of the erg or sentiment that is the source of trouble, including, indeed, a *general* building up of sems at the expense of ergs.

4. Most behaviors, especially in neurosis, have unconscious roots, deriving from a fixation of responses that has taken place in the poor perspective — devoid of experience — of childhood. These fixations must first be brought to consciousness by free association and other methods before being cognitively reintegrated.

5. The shifting of attitudes can take place cognitively only by using the strength of existing sems and new information. It is therefore important that the therapist have, by means of the CAQ, MAT, etc., a clear profile of the patient's makeup, within which the symptom is to be manipulated; he must also gain the patient's concurrence in the arduous therapeutic processes.

Some sem can always be spotted that will offer a reward for a change in attitude. For example, one may need to build up the sem to sport and physical fitness before introducing the cognitive information that makes smoking an undesirable habit. One may need to introduce at the same time a different, substitute narcistic satisfaction, such as chewing gum. The point at which to bring the conflict into cognitive awareness needs to be chosen with care, in relation to the moods of the subject. An inaccurate estimate of the strength of the sems brought into conflict may sometimes produce a backfire in which the wrong sem is defeated ("I would rather give up sports than smoking").

It is assumed above that patient and therapist know the direction in which movement is required. But in the last resort, there are critics who question this fundamental assumption and who claim that we do not know what a "healthy personality" is. Are we to admit that current general practice has not solved the problem of the total *desirable direction of movement in the patient*. Of course, one aims to remove a symptom, but what about the concurrent change of personality? It used to be said that psychologists sometimes cleared up a repression symptom at the cost of producing a socially unbearable personality. [The transition from neurotic to psychopath was well documented by Brunswick (1956) in the days when the superego was considered the villain!]

Implicitly, let us freely admit, one aims to move to a more ideal personality. But what is that? The issue was raised none too soon by White (1973) and responded to by the present writer (1973c), by introducing both measurement of the client and the profile of the society. Every therapist thinks he aims at increasing emotional maturity (C factor), reducing anxiety (QII, $U.I.24$), etc., but White objects that "each individual has his own way of being mature." This misses the mixed action of factors and is as sensible as saying, "Each person has his own way of being heavy." *For a given society there is a definable profile of health.* Ours combines higher scores on some factors (e.g., intelligence, C, G, H, Q_2 and Q_3), lower ones on others (e.g., I, L, M, O, and Q_4), and middle adjustive values on still others (A, D, E, F, H, N, and Q_1). (Though a superficial culture also thinks exvia, A, F, H, and Q_2, should be high.)

Regardless of "agnostic'" assertions, some such profile is implicit in the therapist's procedures, though each has his own ideal, probably to some degree like the therapist's *own* better self. A shift by the patient on a combination of the above traits — based as they are on correlations with most achievements and adjustive behaviors — would be more meaningful than on a single dimension of "getting better." Krug (1984) has recently, from a study of the profiles of all kinds of maladjusted groups, reached a trait profile definition of the "failed personality," giving the negative pole to the dimension we are now searching to define as "desirable."

Most therapy texts also raise another very general issue — the nature of the proper interaction of the personalities of therapist and patient. It might be (there is no research to the contrary) that the formulae found for success in marriage — congeniality and effectiveness — will give us some temporary guidance on this matter. Certainly all writers stress *trust* by the patient (what Freud broadened to "transfer") as clear agreement and alliance on the objectives of therapy, an empathetic sympathy by the therapist, clarity on their respective role boundaries, agreement on responsibility and skill of the therapist, and, of course, legal confidentiality of disclosure. Differences in the personality, beliefs, and appearance of the therapist modify most of these.

Important as the choice of therapist may thus be, he must primarily, like the medical doctor, attach his skills to the scientific values we consider here. This commonly means effectively diagnosing the needs and personality of the patient, directing developmental growth toward health, restructuring personality to remove symptoms, giving assistance with the client's everyday life problems, and agreeing to take the responsibility of temporary "caretaker" action. Except when technicalities are too confusing for the patient, we would generally expect the therapist–patient relation to include the discussion of the intercurrent results on psychological tests; but that also is a subject on which current therapists appreciably disagree. In medicine, also, there are limits to what can be explained to the medically ignorant patient.

Chapter **11**

Strategies in the Structured Learning Therapy of *b*'s and *T*'s

It will by now be clear that the new approach that we call *structured learning therapy* will use several devices that are already embodied in various styles of therapy now in use. Its newness consists in justifying these ad hoc methods in a wider and deeper framework of theory, permitting more apt and intelligent use of them, as well as of newer quantitative methods. Especially, with its precise models, structured learning moves toward that quantitative, psychometric practice that will distinguish scientific, analytical psychotherapist from the rule-of-thumb psychiatrist or psychotherapist.

In the first half of this chapter, we will look at and discuss the methods of a variety of current therapeutic schools, to see how they can fit into the purposes of structured learning therapy. Then, in the second half, we will summarize the objectives and methods finally available in structured learning therapy.

The model of structured learning, as well as the behavioral equation, is a universal one in psychology. All emotional education, in school and in the world, can be represented by the continual change in *b*'s and *s*'s; that is, in the *involvements* of this and that trait, T_x, in life behavior. However, the fact that we deal with common (*R*-

technique) trait forms in our measurements does not deny that they are approximations. For the build-up (or genetics) of a trait in a given individual results in its having *some* degree of uniqueness of form in the individual. Furthermore, for the sake of the pure theorist, we admit that the linear form of the equation may need some nonlinear transformations — found by work with structural equations — in certain cases. But the behavioral equation and the structured learning theory remain the heart of structured learning therapy.

The difference of psychotherapy in general from the normal educational use of structured learning and relearning is that part of it has to deal with attachments and defense mechanisms that are hidden from conscious attachments in pathological behaviors. For Freud, the original events and tie-ups (complexes) in this domain were to be uncovered by tireless free association and dream analysis in the consulting room. For Golden, Perls, and more recent therapists, the method of breaking through by "regression analysis" was to be used so one could go on to other therapies. Regression analysis requires that the patient play the role of being a child again, at the scene (imagined) where the crucial events happened. In this way he experiences the original emotions and sees what needs he has to reconcile with a more holistic, informed adult pattern. For example, he may have been troubled by a sense of guilt toward his mother, which turns out to be due to a chance misunderstanding of the seriousness of a remark by his mother, spoken in distress when her husband told her that the child was responsible for a misdemeanor. Reliving his guilt and depression at this moment he realizes how erroneous it was to take the remark so seriously. Even when exposed, the sense of false guilt may not immediately go away because it is a habit that he feels is part of his "identity." It must be worn away, along with resistance to its admission, by repeated reconsideration. This can often be aided by group therapy.

The overcoming of defense mechanisms is, for various schools of therapy, a major element in the final part of therapy; it calls for the acme of professional skill. Consider the case of the wife who complained that she could not stand the grandiosity and overbearingness of her husband. He seemed unaware of these qualities and denied the instances pointed out to him. In regression therapy he displayed a powerful emotion at recalling a childhood instance when he was humiliated by an older brother. He remembered the incident with shame and also remembered how the same day he began boasting to his mother, which behavior was accepted as a child's "play." The continued regression analyses, in which he struggled to get back to that period of life, brought evidence of the gradual combating of this boasting defense, especially with females. As he recognized the origin of this present-day behavior, he was increasingly able to lessen the overbearingness of which his wife complained.

In another case remedied by regression therapy a man had a hypersensitivity to the barking or nearness of dogs. A recollection of play at four years of age unearthed an incident in which the family dog had bitten him. He could recall permanganate being poured over his bitten arm and his distress at thinking it was blood. Then he guiltily recalled that he had been tugging at the dog's tail and that he was initially angry at the dog's response. The anger and guilt had to come out (reluctantly) before he was able to hear dogs barking without any subconscious sense of fear.

The present popularity of cognitive therapy is undoubtedly a return in part to a pre-Freudian Victorian belief in "reasonableness." It had its most flagrant expression years ago in Korzybsky's arguments that people are psychotic because they have a wrong meaning for words, and can be brought to health by relearning their correct meanings. The truth in cognitive therapy is that emotions and actions *are* set off by cognitive stimuli. Authoritative persuasion can often convince a person that, say, his conception of a boss as a threat is false. But, as the obstinate beliefs of Communists, Republicans, and Democrats show, redirection by reasoning is a difficult process. Usually the success of a cognitive approach requires, first, a good understanding of the client's dynamic lattice. As a student, he may have accepted a Marxist position because his most esteemed friends were Marxists. A cognitive demonstration of the economic errors in Marxist theory comes into conflict with these earlier loyalties. Part of the cognitive shift requires getting those loyalties into perspective as adolescent emotional experiences.

There *are* dynamic readjustments that can be brought about by bringing rational cognitive substitution in the dynamic lattice, as described earlier. But we must recognize, as above, that there are many instances where the link in the dynamic lattice is unconscious, as Freud first pointed out. To bring an impulse under cognitive manipulation, the origin — the learned link — must be made available to consciousness by one of the devices of regression therapy: acting out at a childhood level, free association, dreams, hypnotism, and perhaps in the future by drugs. *All* behavior has its "irrational reasons" in hidden links, but it is mainly in neurosis that the magnified and forgotten early experience causes links that are hard to dispel or adjust to by ordinary reasoning.

Let us consider next what can be called "diversion" therapy. When the erg with a disproportionate and peculiar expression is an appetitive one, a commonsense examination of the lattice suggests that the disproportional expression may be weakened by opening up *other* behaviors motivated by that same erg. This cognitively simple "solution" has been attempted by attaching homosexual men to attractive women, but has succeeded with only a minority. Yet in principle it is an aid, requiring for full success that steps be taken to attack the original cause of the perverse outlet that has been set up. Diversion techniques help; in the above case of the dominating husband, such diversionary outlets could be found in his military career. With this two-sided attack — regression and diversion — the domestic problem in the above case was greatly ameliorated and in time disappeared.

We have agreed that the patient normally comes to the therapist with a *problem*, which is primarily one of dissatisfaction and can be placed and indexed on the APA Chart (Figure 9.1). Although the therapist often helps the relearning with suggestions regarding useful environmental effects from maneuvers in the actual life situation, the effects of environment are commonly in the past and must be handled by "internal" therapy with the patient. Nevertheless, many therapists give much thought to reducing stimuli in the environment — especially with patients who are children — and to engineering a better learning and adaptation situation. For such engineering to be really dependable the therapist needs to know objectively the vector of a given cause in a given environment. As explained when dealing above with the concept of the *situational vector*, clinical research has, as yet, provided evidence on very few.

Finally, we come to look at existing practices for changing trait levels — as dynamic traits, general personality traits, and abilities. For every patient the therapist normally, after diagnosis and appraisal of the environment, needs to enter into a clear (but revisable) treatment plan. Such differential therapy involves considering the tactics of the dozen or so specific types of intervention now in use. It also involves concern for the general goal of the tactics, for the given patient. Is one dealing with an *acute* case of comparatively sudden environmental attack (and perhaps involving legal action)? Or a case needing rehabilitation after earlier previous treatment? Or a case calling for steady maintenance of treatment? Or a case calling only for passing on to the client a self-helping diagnosis? Goals and methods interact.

In discussing cases with practicing therapists, one cannot help realizing that there is now a good proportion that are essentially nonpathological — people who simply need help, as from a friend, with some minor problem. It is for these that the numerous self-help paperbacks appear on "How to make friends," "How to be successful in marriage," "How to concentrate on job promotion," and so on. One is astonished to see such a naiveté, which did not exist in those brought up in a middle-class family that taught its children these skills as part of their upbringing. In these cases, the therapist is simply teaching skills, values, and relatively obvious solutions that one would expect the client's common sense already to be aware of. This advent of "social and personal teaching" in the psychotherapeutic world, as a departure from handling true pathologies, seems to have passed unnoticed in the preparation of the therapist to meet changing demands. In any case, such work is, in the broad sense, directed to changing ability traits, e.g., social intelligence, general educational level, and is well understood.

Returning to neurotic patients, one notes that many have a *specific* symptom, whose treatment calls for no major alteration of trait levels as such. This is where reflexological (behavioristic) methods will often suffice. (See note 8 in Chapter 9.) But many cases of social maladaptation or marital difficulties undoubtedly call for the modification of level of a whole personality unitary trait or traits. The realistic therapist recognizes that the changing of level of an entire T—be it a general personality trait or a dynamic sem or erg—calls for a different strategy from the above. But first and foremost, the structured learning theorist simply has to inquire to what extent behavior genetics and life curve data show that the trait in question *is* susceptible to environmental change. Moreover, one must not forget that the choice of which trait needs alteration requires a study of the behavioral equation b's for the particular symptom behavior concerned.

The genetic evidence on the relative determination by heredity is now available for most primary and secondary traits and states, and knowledge of it should be part of any psychologist's training. The recent evidence of behavior genetics is that intelligence, B, surgency, F, and premsia-vs-harria, I, are greatly determined by heredity, while dominance, E, super ego, G, boldness-shyness, H, conservatism, Q_1, and ergic tension, Q_4, are, contrariwise, greatly susceptible to environmental molding. Since intelligence is a central and much discussed source trait, let it be added that crystallized intelligence is much more subject to environment than is fluid intelligence, and that in particular areas and in adult life it shows appreciable response to training. The possible change in g_c in a middle-aged person, through broadening of interests, should thus not be ruled out; but no great change is to be expected—except downward, through physiological injury—in fluid intelligence, g_f.

A trait that is heavily innate, such as B (g_f), F, and I on the CAQ, or, in the O–A battery series, $U.I.$ 16, 19, 24 (anxiety), and 25 (Cattell, 1981), is still likely to be susceptible to physiological medication change (as with Valium or Miltown on $U.I.$ 24). Our whole treatment to this point has concentrated on dynamics and leaves medication to the specialist psychiatrist, though we touch on it briefly in the next chapter. However, we must emphasize, in passing, that our basic diagnostic procedures are also vital to medication treatment and call for cooperation of psychotherapist and psychiatrist in handling the matter. For example, there are six or seven distinctive depression traits with corresponding scales evidenced in the CAQ. Unfortunately, no psychiatric research has yet used this factor analytic revelation to study which of the forms of trait or state depression respond best to which pharmaceuticals. A beginning has been made in the work of Neal (see Krug, 1977b), with his DI/AN formula. These letters correspond to antidepressives desipramine, imipramine, amitriptyline, and nortriptyline. He found a personality difference on the 16 PF that differentiates those who respond to DI from those who respond to AN. Expressed quantitatively, it is DI/AN = $H - Q_2 + Q_3$, and he supplies norms for prediction thereby.

The principal source traits on which therapeutic change is most often called for are sizothymia, A, ego strength, C, dominance, E' superego, G, boldness, H, protension, L, self-esteem vs. guilt (and unworthiness), O, ergic tension, Q_4, and some of the depressions, D_1 through D_7, in the CAQ.

The evidence for change on dominance is as expected — that positions of power and responsibility increase it, and that it usually rises from a subnormal to a normal level during psychotherapy. Ego strength similarly increases in successful psychotherapy, presumably as a result of reward from greater self-command (Cattell, Rickels, et al., 1966). Superego strength has been shown normally to increase in successful marriage, in belonging to church circles, and in occupying positions of administrative authority.

A good deal of attention has been given to the H (boldness-vs.-shyness) factor in the attempts to remedy excessive shyness, e.g., by Lowenstein (1954). Zimbardo, for example, has shown that by inducing persons to act out in nonshy ways, i.e., changing the b's in shy behavior by provocation, a positive change in the trait usually occurs, although a minority react in the opposite direction. H, which we understand as the balance of parasympathetic to sympathetic system reactivity, obviously has a physiological, partly genetic basis (as is shown, for example, by its shift under alcohol and other drugs). But the genetic research shows environment nevertheless to predominate. It also increases for the average person throughout life (Cattell, 1975) as a result of reassuring experiences or physiological change. In any case, it can be psychologically shifted away from shyness by such changes in the b's of its expression as Zimbardo and others have explored.

Change in the O factor is important, especially in connection with anxiety, in which it is an important primary. In its negative (low) score, it corresponds (with an admixture of Q_3) to the popular concept of "self-esteem." In its positive (high) score, it is a sense of worthlessness and guilt such as is involved in many profound religious experiences. In its high O score, it is frequently involved in pathologies, and the therapist commonly does well to try to lower it.

There has recently been a movement in psychotherapy to attempts to increase self-esteem, e.g., among Rogerians and by Frey and Carlock (1984). Since the term is given only a popular meaning and is largely, as far as can be precisely determined, a mixture of $O(-)$, H, and Q_3, plus some E (dominance), it is not possible to find precise research (with the CAQ, MAT, etc.) to back up the assertions made about therapeutic importance and treatment of such a trait mixture. In addition, the possibility seems to be rarely considered that one can have too much of $O(-)$ for good social adjustment and that in normal persons it usually reaches a level appropriate to the person's talents and life position. Certainly we do not yet have positive evidence on what experiences modify O and Q_3. There is evidence that high O individuals suffered deficient love and attention as children. Much that Erikson writes about under the categories "faith" and "self-trust" has to do with O. High O experiences are clearly what is involved in William James's "dark night of the soul," and being "reborn" religiously is a substitution of love of and by God for the missing human experience. The therapist might well aid this sense of being reborn. The person with high O typically has a low C score (this is one of the highest primary trait intercorrelations). But the low O behavior is not entirely healthy either and has been noted to be rigid, with an excess of defense mechanisms. Thus a declining score on O, in the course of monitoring, is a good therapeutic sign, though it is questionable whether a *very* low O score is desirable socially, as just mentioned.

Pursuing the above list of modifiable source traits to the end, we come to Q_4, which is frustration, with manifestations of excessive autonomic reactivity.[9] Along with $C(-)$, O, L, and $Q_3(-)$, a high Q_4 score constitutes a high score on the *second-order anxiety fac-*

tor, Q II, which almost all therapy aims to reduce. The "emergent" theory of anxiety (p. 68) is that of interaction in which low C causes unused (unexpressed) drive to accumulate in Q_4, thus raising Q_4; Q_4 in turn weakens C by depriving it of ergic expression and demand for defense mechanisms against this stress. However, there is evidence of some genetic influence in Q_4, in the form of a high inherited *autonomic* responsiveness. The reduction of Q_4 clearly involves the provision of new ergic outlets acceptable to C, and there is evidence that it shows marked decline if outlets are provided. It also declines through the physiological effect of tranquilizers.

In dealing with trait change we have confined ourselves to those traits revealed as primaries through the factoring of questionnaires and behavior ratings. By contrast to the 16 PF traits, too much mystery still surrounds the ten personality traits measured in the O–A battery — except *U.I.* 24 (anxiety), *U.I.* 23 (regression), *U.I.* 21 (exuberance), *U.I.* 17 (control), and *U.I.* 19 (independence). The disposition of these in *diagnosis* is tolerably known, but experimental evidence of change is still scant.

Compared to normal controls neurotics are higher on *U.I.* 24 (anxiety), *U.I.* 23 (regression), and *U.I.* 32 (introversion); they are lower on *U.I.* 16 (ego standards), *U.I.* 19 (independence), and *U.I.* 21 (exuberance). As to schizophrenia, a highly diagnostic weighted composite can be made from *U.I.* 16 – , *U.I.* 19 – , *U.I.* 21 – , *U.I.* 23 – , *U.I.* 25 – , *U.I.* 30 – , *U.I.* 32 – , and *U.I.* 33. It will be noted that *U.I.* 25 (inner tension), *U.I.* 30 (somindence), and *U.I.* 33 (discouragement) are extra, in schizophrenia, to the neurotic deviations. This relatively powerful discriminating capacity of the O–A kit suggests that it be used when, as frequently happens, there is doubt about a schizophrenic diagnosis.

The diagnostic differentiations by discriminant functions are usually greater with the O–A than the CAQ [or any other questionnaire, as Schmidt and Hacker (1984) have shown], despite the unknown naming of some factors in the former. For example, Patrick, Cattell, Price, and Campbell (1981) found a weighted combination of *U.I.* 19, *U.I.* 20, *U.I.* 25, and *U.I.* 30 correctly classified 74% of the depressives and 83% of the normals in one out-patient department.

Clear evidence of a combination of therapy and chemotherapy to shift scores on these factors is shown by the psychiatric research of Cattell, Rickels, et al. (1966). In Table 11.1 the changes on two O–A source traits were set out along with consistent, concomitant results on the 16 PF verbal measure of the same trait, anxiety (second-order factor Q II and *U.I.* 24). The gains in O–A source trait measures through the ordinary therapies are significant from the .05 to .001 levels. There is indeed much ground today for greater "blind" use of the O–A battery source traits in diagnosis, in the sense that although the meaning of some of them is still unknown, they are very potent in diagnosis and prediction of change under therapy (see Table 11.1). (Note also the change on the O–A regression factor, *U.I.* 23.)

In conclusion, we see that there is already much evidence that

TABLE 11.1 Measurable Changes in *U.I.* 23, Mobilization-vs.-Regression, and *U.I.* 24, Anxiety Produced by Therapy (Comparison of Anxiety and Regression Change Under Therapy on Questionnaire and Objective Test Measures[a])

	Initial score (1)	Final score (2)	Change (2) – (1)
IPAT verbal anxiety			
($N = 46$) Patients	46.09	43.02	– 3.07[c]
($N = 53$) Controls	26.13	26.77	0.64
O-A anxiety battery			
Patients[b]	0.361	0.198	– 0.163[c]
Controls	– 0.361	– 0.472	– 0.111
O-A regression battery			
Patients	0.440	0.114	– 0.326[d]
Controls	– 0.458	– 0.611	– 0.153[c]

Note: Results from Cattell, Rickels, and others (1966), *American J. Psychotherapy, 20,* 281–269.

[a]$N = 46$ patients, 53 normal controls.

[b]Numerical agreement of these two initial values for patients and controls is accidental. All scores are raw scores and have no comparability immediately from objective to questionnaire values, being unstandardized.

[c]Significant at $p < 0.05$.

[d]Significant at $p < 0.001$.

measured trait levels can be significantly altered by therapy of various kinds. It happens in part through removal of defense mechanisms that in effect prevent a trait's natural development, and in part through attachment of trait expressions to new domains and larger b values. In the latter case, the engineering of behavioral expression of a trait, e.g., of H, before the person is spontaneously ready to make the new expression can often begin by experiencing some "accidentally" satisfactory b expression, which, rewarded, causes growth.

In considering the strategy and meaning of b and T changes, it behooves us also to look in more detail into practical tactics. Some discussion is particularly needed of the cognitive approach in structured learning theory. Learning in animals, by either the classical, CR I, coexcitation (classical conditioning) method or by means–end, CR II (instrumental conditioning) has been largely studied in physical behavior. In man, the enormous development of intelligence and ideation makes the same processes, at the ideational level, almost unrecognizable, and, until recently, was systematically little used.

In classical conditioning two stimuli are brought together physically perhaps half-a-dozen times to produce a common reaction — a new response to the conditioned stimulus. With man's ideational capacity and his constant kaleidoscope of ideas, they can be brought together a thousand times in the course of a day. Our ordinary associations of ideas are in part brought about by the familiar coexcitation present in classical conditioning, CR I. The "associationists" of the eighteenth and nineteenth centuries thus had already recognized and ordered the principle in Pavlov's, Watson's, and Skinner's rules of conditioning. We must recognize, however, that additional determiners of association come from emotional production and mental-set production of the associate response. That a thought about taxes follows a thought about earning more money derives from some emotional, dynamic connection other than simple coexcitation. That the thought "black" follows the thought "white" derives from a common mental tendency to educe opposites, though sheer past coexcitation may also play a part.

The high frequency with which, in thought, all our ideas become coexcited, makes the origin of thought sequences by unusual degrees of past coexcitation quite minor. Dynamic and mental-set considerations usually prevail. Structured learning heeds this fact. If we want the thought of liking a drink to become connected with an action other than drinking, we can suggest the new connection and it may recur, with perhaps some guidance, a hundred times during the day and tend to become established by internal classical conditioning. For coexcitation is a matter of the patient's committing to memory two stimulus ideas, which his brain can firmly connect, given the correct cue. It requires a dynamic commitment, however, which the patient normally cannot maintain without the therapist's periodic intervention and the marshaling of a dynamic set. Sheer cognitive intervention is not enough.

The second of our five learning principles from Chapter 1, by which the patient learns by experiencing a reward (CR II), requires, if it is to grow automatically, a perusal by the therapist of the individual's dynamic profile (of semic and ergic strengths) to see from which dynamic sources rewards can best be drawn. The therapist needs to perceive which are the strongest sems and which are presently the least expressed (highest U score, lowest I score) ergs. The tactic becomes a matter of seeing which can best be brought into action to provide a motive where one is needed or to block a motive that is problematic. This requires some subsequent trial-and-error exploration of the dynamic profiles to see if response comes as expected.

For example, consider a child of good intelligence who is not doing well in school. The SMAT score shows he has a low school sentiment but a high sem to sport and to the parental home. Can one enlist these latter in school work? Some fairly prolonged discussions with the client are necessary, in which he comes to see that his success in school is important to his parents. This may help build up a school sentiment that subsidiates to his parental, home sentiment. At the same time he may be brought to realize that the self-assertive drive, in the sports sentiment, can also be used to achieve satisfaction by means of preeminence in school work.

If we follow Bandura, James, McDougall, and others we recognize that imitation and the following of suggestions depend to some extent on admiration for the guide or adviser. Presumably the therapist — with the patient's "transfer" — can maintain his own status usefully, but he needs to discover in the patient's life persons the client does or can admire to use as a model. The growth of sentiments is appreciably built on admired models — real and fictional.

Much sentiment growth in early life is spontaneous, springing from chance behavior that has become chance rewarded. Thus one child, happening to pick up some fascinating book, begins a voyage through many further books to a whole sentiment toward reading. Another does well on a first ride on a horse, and becomes fascinated with horses and horse riding. These are the circumstantial events that the therapist uses to understand the case and also, to some extent, to introduce as guides.

We have accepted that the patient comes to the therapist with a *problem*, which is primarily one of dissatisfaction, and can be placed and indexed on the APA Chart (Figure 9.1). Although the therapist often helps with suggestions regarding maneuvers in the actual life situation, the problem has, by the time of entrance into therapy, probably moved on to neurotic inner responses at crossroads (chiasms) D, E, and F. It needs the unearthing of childhood responses and much else described above. But in true psychotherapy (as distinct from conditioning work on a narrow behavioral symptom) one must not overlook the fact that strengthening of the ego, C, factor is needed in virtually all pathologies. There is usually also a need for coincident reduction of anxiety. This tends always to accompany low C on the second-order factors $C-$, L, O, Q_3-, and Q_4. This C increase is a universally needed change in specific therapies of all kinds.

To strengthen the ego it is necessary to give it repeated victories over impulse and mood. These need to be arranged and pointed out to the patient as evidence of progress. The places where conflicts may be sought in a given patient are indicated in the MAT by large U, relative to I, scores on the given interest. Improvement of C strength (integration) thus lies partly in finding real-life outlets for what is lying unintegrated in the U measures of various dynamic traits. For example, a person with a relatively large U on the gregarious erg is missing social life and contacts, probably through some early trauma or a low score on the personality factor H. Life expression in some club or in sociable novel reading are indicated. Every increase shown in the MAT monitoring retest on I score, relative to U scores, is a contribution to increase on the C factor. For C is measurable (Cattell, 1985) as the reduction of conflict-produced impairment of the cognitive connections at the pathways to the ultimate ergic springs.

With the completion of the part of this chapter that surveys methods of treatment, we may now turn to a final summary of the principles of structured learning theory, condensing and putting in perspective what has gone before.

First let us return to the assertion that two and only two modifications can be made in therapy: changing b's and changing T's.

The first modification involves changing b's, behavioral indices, and the involvements, v's, and modulators, s's, they contain. The v's are matters of practice and largely concern weights on abilities in the broadest sense of ability, expressing their role in effective action.

Changing s's, describes the satisfaction in situations and courses of action since they indicate how much the dynamic trait is habitually excited and modified in level by contact with the situation. The excitement that the situation causes is dependent on all five learning laws, e.g., CR I and CR II, but especially on the reward in CR II, means–end (ME) learning.

This may sometimes require the therapist to persuade the client to the course of action before the latter believes there will be any reward to it. *Experience* can best prove the existence of a stabilizing reward. In general, however, the structured learning principles require the therapist to scout out the possible *internal* rewards on the basis of the measurement of personality structures ready to seek reward, and particularly the form of the subsidiation that one can work out in the client's dynamic lattice.

One must not overlook that the required change in s's also means *undoing* (relearning and deconditioning) as well as learning, and this requires a knowledge of the older, unconscious links in the dynamic lattice (the child within the adult). Where these are *common* trait links, as in the Oedipus complex or in Jung's archetypes, they will be known to the therapist from the ordinary R-technique revelation of the common lattice in our culture, for R-technique with objective motivation measurement devices reveals unconscious as well as conscious subsidiation.[11] But with complexes that are unique, the connection can be reliably, but at great cost, revealed by P-technique, or, less reliably, by Freudian techniques of free association, dream analysis, humor tests, etc.

The expiration of a socio-psychologically undesirable expression, i.e., a symptom, is attempted in reflexological (behavioristic) practice by constant repetition of the stimulus without the feared consequence and generally with an arranged positive reward. But in structured learning theory one traces the subsidiations in the lattice, i.e., discerns the motivation and encourages several alternative paths to the ergic goal that will in due course attenuate the motivation of the undesirable expression.

Regarding the diagnostic estimation of b (v and s) weights, which will normally hold for half-a-dozen behaviors central to the patient's problem, we must unfortunately repeat that the slowness of research leaves the theoretical clarity of structured learning empirically in the lurch. We do not know the R-technique weights for more than a few behaviors, and the P-technique approach is presently too time-consuming for the average patient. The fact must therefore be faced that the alternative "methods of clinical estimation of trait involvement" must presently be left to the therapists skills.

The second modification involves the reduction and increase of trait scores. Fortunately, in getting trait (and state) scores we are already on a firm foundation. The principal primary ability traits are measured in the CAB (Hakstian, 1976; Hakstian, Thorndike, and Cattell, 1976), and the personality sphere of behavior has been the basis for the 16 PF, CAQ, HSPQ, CPQ, and the children's versions in the ESPQ and PSPQ. It has been shown (Boyle, 1985) that the dynamic trait measurement in the MAT and SMAT is out in "new space" beyond the 16 PF, CAQ general personality traits, and, again, that the *state* axes in the Curran 8-State Questionnaire are independent of trait scores. The practicing psychologist therefore has today a magnificent array of confirmed independent trait state measures available for diagnosis.

A decision resting more in "art" concerns which traits — ability, temperamental, and dynamic — the therapist needs to work on in each client, and by what methods he can modify the trait (or state). The bases for choice of traits to work on have already been indicated. The dynamic traits are always modifiable, but genetic research shows that such traits as F, I, and B (intelligence) must be regarded as relatively fixed. In general, ego strength (C in the 16 PF and CAQ) will be a trait on which the most work will be needed. As stated, psychology as a science has only very recently begun to show which common traits are susceptible to change and how change may be effected. (We must accept the opinion of psychoanalysts and reflexologists that *unique* traits are being altered by therapy.) [11]

Let us here survey what experiment and theory yet exist about the ways of modifying common traits. It is necessary not only to show change, but also to show that change comes to a *unitary* whole, as such. The *dR* researches of Kameoka (1986) on the CAQ and Cattell on the 16 PF (1963) show clearly that when trait levels alter they tend to alter on all elements at once. But let us ask how this occurs, according to structured learning theory.

(a) *By manipulating specific life paths and situations.* Over a period of two to four years one can produce changes that can definitely be linked to specific path experience. The work of Cattell and Barton (1972, 1975) shows, for example, that marriage tends to raise superego (G factor), that prolonged illness lowers E (dominance) and F (surgency), that success in career raises E (dominance) and C (ego strength), that college attendance raises radicalism (Cattell, Barton, and Vaughan, 1973), and so on. These findings can be brought to relatively precise calculation of the complex effects, for guidance of therapy by situation, by means of matrices in the *path learning analysis* model (p. 99) and *adjustment process analysis* chart (p. 103). All learning is "multidimensional change in a multidimensional situation," and only by matrices can the complexities of change from a new situation or therapy be intelligently followed (see Cattell, Dielman, and Barton, 1973, 1974). However, apart from using measured evidence of what common life paths will do to traits, the therapist can make educated guesses, from his knowledge of traits

TABLE 11.2. Qualification Weighting Grid for Estimating Effectiveness as Retail (Route) Salesman Using Curvilinear Relations

	Personality Factor															
	A	B	C	E	F	G	H	I	L	M	N	O	Q_1	Q_2	Q_3	Q_4
Stens for given Individual:																
Sten Score							*Weights*									
10	8	0	0	0	2	0	2	0	0	0	2	0	0	8	7	0
9	9	0	1	1	2	0	4	1	1	0	2	0	0	9	7	0
8	10	1	2	2	3	0	5	2	2	0	3	1	0	10	6	1
7	9	2	3	3	3	0	7	2	4	0	3	2	0	9	5	2
6	8	3	2	4	2	1	6	2	5	1	2	2	1	7	4	3
5	6	4	2	4	2	2	4	2	6	2	1	2	2	6	4	4
4	4	3	2	5	1	2	3	2	8	2	2	1	2	4	3	6
3	2	2	1	6	0	1	2	1	7	3	1	1	2	3	2	8
2	1	1	0	5	0	1	1	0	6	2	0	0	2	1	1	6
1	0	0	0	4	0	0	0	0	4	0	0	0	1	0	0	4
Weight (for given individual):																

Total Weighted Score (for given individual)_____

Qualification Level. _____

Source: From *Handbook for the Sixteen Personality Factor Questionnaire (16 PF)*, p. 155, by R. B. Cattell, H. W. Eber, and M. Tatsuoka, 1970. Champaign, IL: Institute for Personality and Ability Testing.

and the biographical evidence from the patient, of changes in traits that might be handled by bringing about situation change, e.g., of type of job, marriage, and so forth.

Our basic survey of structure and principles shows what avenues to such change are possible. Attachment to a certain institution, e.g., church, home, career, will, we know, bring about changes by the environment manipulation means above, utilizing the first principle — of *common frequency* of exposure. It is rare that an influence cannot be found and evoked from the environment in the case of most clients, and a good therapist uses all of them, from school to Alcoholics Anonymous.

(b) *By cognitive and other manipulation in the consulting room*. Psychotherapies of various kinds have begun to assess their degrees of success. A specific instance is the significant reduction of anxiety, Q II and *U.I.* 24, obtained by psychoanalysis in the study of middle-class patients by Cattell, Rickels, et al. (1966). The same study showed an even more marked reduction of the O–A battery factor *U.I.* 23 (regression), now better understood in its associations (Cattell and Schuerger, 1982).

The same reductions of anxiety and regression and increase of ego strength have been recorded from other methods, notably the cognitive reconstruction of perceptions that we have advocated as an important tool in therapy of less severe cases. In the evidence of trait-level change by manipulation in the consulting room, using imagery, by cognitive discussion pointing out new possible paths, without psychoanalytic transference, we should include particularly the recent demonstrations of changes in dynamic traits from cognitive reattachments. There is, however, no evidence of the degree of permanence of these changes.

One must also consider the production of significant and unitary changes on *state* levels. Kawash, Dielman, and Cattell (1972), Cattell, Kawash, and DeYoung (1973), Cattell, Barton, and Kawash (1972), and Cattell, DeYoung, Gaborit, and Barton (1973) show that the ergic tension levels on fear, sex, thirst, and others change significantly with exposure to such stimuli as a movie, a laboratory on fire, deprivation of satisfaction, and so on. They change as unitary wholes. Brennan (1983), Curran (1976), Boyle (1983a), and others have shown that twenty minutes of movie stimuli produce highly significant changes similar on seven of the states on the 8-State Battery. These are unitary states, and one would expect such change. But Griffith and Rogers (1976) and Kohen et al. (1982) find little effect of these temporary state stimuli on drinking and driving habits. States must be regarded as what they are — temporary deviations — but it is nevertheless important to see how stimuli affect states in a given person.

Setting aside the effects on true general states (e.g., depression, arousal), we nevertheless find results on ergs and sentiments that we may expect to be more permanent. Thus Boyle (1984) found effects of a traffic accident movie on MAT measures, as shown in Table 11.3.

The ergic tension measures — Nos. 2, 3, and 6 in Table 11.3 — we expect, from formulation (5.1), p. 56, to be *temporarily* responsive to stimulus pressures. But it may well be that the changes in sems — Nos. 1, 5, and 7 — have some permanent residue. At least, common observation tells us that a single painful or pleasurable experience is known to change a person's views and sentiments for life. The Boyle (and other similar) data suggest that the existence of "esthetic distance" in viewing movies or plays does not deny the value of more extensive use of these aids in altering traits by consulting-room means. At least this is true of dynamic traits (sems) though it remains to be investigated in general personality (style) traits as in the 16 PF, CAQ, etc.

(c) *Change of trait score by reward.* Elsewhere (Cattell, 1980a, 1981) we have formulated three processes through which the *unitary* character of a sem is raised by use of the five structured learning principles. They are (1) common frequency and intensity of learning among the attitudes involved in the sem, (2) spread of an agency

TABLE 11.3 Changes in Ergs and Sems from Stimulating Movie Situation

MAT factor	F value of change		P value
1. Career sem (unintegrated)	4.21	(–)	.04
2. Unintegrated fear	30.59	(+)	.00001
3. Integrated fear	16.29	(+)	.0002
4. Integrated narcism	5.38	(–)	.02
5. Integrated superego	6.59	(+)	.01
6. Unintegrated mating	6.59	(–)	.01
7. Unintegrated sweetheart	1.73	(–)	u.s

Source: From Effects of viewing a road trauma film on emotional and motivational factors. *Individual Differences and Personality 4*, pp. 1–7, by G. J. Boyle, 1984.

by internal thought as in (b) above, and (3) *budding*, or growth through a common dynamic investment, in subsidiating to reward on another preexisting unitary dynamic trait. We are less concerned here with explaining growth as a unit than in explaining growth as such, but we may pause to examine these processes.

The first is easily understood and explained in reflexology. Social institutions, e.g., church, school, job, involve a whole *set* of attitudes, not necessarily dynamically or even logically connected, but all exercised to the same degree. A person brought up in a church, compared to one who is not, will sing hymns, listen to sermons, pray, give money to the church, etc. — all with a greater learning exposure. The result, in a mixed group, will be a unitary factor of a religious sem. The therapist may affect by (a) and (b) above only one or two attitudes in a sem, but by so doing he raises its score on the whole.

By agency action we mean a dynamic growth akin to what Piaget saw in the ability field. The individual's discovery of a single principle, e.g., causality, will become widely employed and bring a common growth of several cognitive habits. The same can happen with a dynamic agency, e.g., a discovery of what empathy does in helping us understand others. Doubtless this spread of a single "agency" depends on the existence of a good deal of internal thought, as well as trial-and-error experiment. But the raising of a unitary sem to one's country (patriotism) or to one's self (the self-sentiment) is spread through many subsidiating attitudes by the individual's thought and experience in regard to a discovered sem object. In this we should include the effect of modeling on an admired person (as studied by Bandura, 1962, and insightfully discussed by McDougall, 1932) in rewarding growth. In this case the unitary character of a whole series of particular attitudes reflects the unitariness of traits in the admired person. Raising a sentiment by the *agency* principle is what many therapists do in the consulting room, but rather blindly, by such methods as cognitive psychology, regression (in an undoing of an agency), and group therapy (to build into the self-sentiment). In all forms the approach involves conscious appreciation of the goal of the sem, and an awareness of what ergs can be brought into action to build it up. In the case of raising ego strength, C, for example, a discussion of (1) its value as a means to this and that goal, through capacity to persevere, and (2) of the anatomy of C as discussed in the five steps on p. 84 are called for.

The third source of unitariness in a sem is a common dynamic strength, paralleling the common frequency of exercise mentioned above as the first of two ways to effect a modification in therapy. This assumes that frequency and motivation strength are the two main determiners of learning. If a person has a well-developed sem to his career, and suddenly computers become important to it, he is likely to develop a smaller "computer sem" subsidiated to the reward of career. All the various attitudes and skills in the computer sem will tend to be learned together and to the same degree because of subsidiation to the same (career) reward — creating a unitary factor where individual differences are factored.

The therapist may wonder why the trouble is taken here to explain the rise of a *unitary* factor pattern. A fair amount of learning is specific, increasing the strength of a particular attitude. One can only reply that in the interest of *economy*, amid thousands of specific attitudes, we do well economically to deal with the fewer ergs and sems that show up in most people as unitary traits, as in the 16 PF, MAT, CAQ, etc.

That the similarity of R and dR factors means a common *arousal*, on a genetically-determined set of connections in the parts of an erg, is reasonably certain. But does it mean, in the case of a sem, that there is common cognitive *activation* of all the attitudes loaded in the factor when one or two of them are stimulated? The evidence so far suggests that, at least to an appreciable degree, the cue stimulating one part of the cognitive network that bounds a particular sem awakens the retrievability of the other attitudes found in the factor. We are entitled, from the dR results, to believe that raising any attitude in a sem or discussing the goal of a sem will tend to raise its level *as a whole*. Incidentally, here we run into the technical question raised earlier of whether a change produced in the b in a particular attitude (or set of attitudes) is a contributor to raising the total sem score. Higher b's also raise the *accuracy* of estimation of a sem score, from adding attitudes. The trained therapist, looking at the client's profile on the CAQ, MAT, and perhaps also the 8 SQ (8-State Questionnaire) in relation to the life situation and the symptoms will have decided that improvement will rest in part on *lowering* some highly deviant traits as well as raising others. Regarding abolition of sentiments, the therapist should be reminded that the Freudian concept of unconscious complexes remains a firm truth, and amid more generalized modern practices the need remains to bring these dynamic entities into consciousness and remodification by older (Freudian) and newer (regression analysis) principles (see note 1). One needs to bring this client back, in imagination, to his childhood and let him relive and realize the conflict he then had and the defenses he adopted. As yet, despite Wenig's (Cattell and Wenig, 1952) basic research, we have no psychometric measures of defenses, except as they associate with factors like L (projection defense) and M (fantasy) on the 16 PF or CAQ. However, the repeated consulting-room exposure, with the client's insight, of defenses from childhood operating in existing traits will reduce them to control and disappearance, by the agency principle of sem modification.

As to the third principle — "budding," the common growth of trait elements through the service of a common motive — we may note that but for the inhibitions of civilized life this would simply lead to a set of attitudes developed around each ergic goal. We are concerned here, however, with the "civilized" expectation of a new sem developing in the service of an established sem and of an erg. Much of the energy of the erg will uniformly affect all the new semic attitudes learned. An individual with a strong sweetheart attachment may develop a previously nonexistent sem to a steady career, or a person with a strong career sem may develop a sentiment to learning the principles of, say, banking or computer use that will subsidiate to success in the career. This is where a knowledge of existing sem strengths and distributions on the MAT scores will be of particular value to the therapist. Granted that he knows reliably where the most powerful sems lie, he can see where to develop new subsidiary sems of advantage in adjustment.

Since we have stressed that the growth of C factor, ego strength, is the most important common requirement, let us pause to discuss the process. Heather Cattell (1986) has found value in direct training of each of the five panels found to be active (p. 84). But there are various additional means. First, the therapist may, with great discretion, seek to unlock the energy tied up in defense mechanisms. The adult ego may be able to withstand what the childhood ego could not. If $L+$ and $O-$ are evidence of defenses, it may be possible to explore with persons high on these where the defenses began.

The main principle in strengthening the ego, however, is for the individual to gain reward experience of success in controlling impulse. It has been shown that even experience of effects of a tranquilizer, in giving control of emotionality, raises C. But the alert perception by the therapist of gains demonstrable to the client will — especially with good transfer — prove the reward the client needs. This growth of C may also be initiated by admired characters, strong in C factor, provided the gap is not so great as to be impracticable. The therapist's precise knowledge (e.g., through the MAT profile) of what strong sentiments may be brought into alliance with the ego in controlling ergic swings will help the patient muster control — especially during the period when the growth of the ego is uncertain.

NOTES

[9]Although multivariate behavioral research has given, in factors C and G, support and extension to the psychoanalytic concepts of the ego and superego structures, it has been silent, as pointed out above, on Freud's third idea — the id (except in motivation component α). As a basic, given entity in all human beings, the possibility exists that it does not *vary* enough to yield, by R- or P-technique, a differentiating factor. In objective dynamic measures a factor of narcism appears strongly, and some resemblance to the id may be said to exist in its strong negative correlation (-32 to -60) with the superego. But it is not negative with the self-sentiment, is only .15 with autism, and has consistent positive correlation with some social success criteria. Early studies, however, seriously considered the possibility of a narcism-superego, head and tail, opposition. It was also considered that the second-order *control* factor (Q VIII, $U.I.$ 17) might be the obverse of the id; but everything points to the C, $F(-)$, G, and Q_3 second order being an acquired feature.

A second direction in which one might look would be for a single second-order factor covering all the ergs. The analysis by Krug and Cattell (1971) and Boyle (1984), however, give a surprising complex picture of the second order in the MAT. Krug (1981) took low fear, high pugnacity and conflict, and high superego as the best measures of criminal personality. Boyle's technically fine study in particular yields nine second-order factors, among which are high integrated pugnacity with low fear, narcism, and self-sentiment; another of high career with low mating, self-sentiment, and unintegrated pugnacity; and another with high mating and low narcism, which fits the pattern that Birkett & Cattell found productive of alcoholism, as an attempt at solution of problems, and a guide to where solutions appear to be blocked. It does, however, suggest that the disguises are more accidental than Freud supposed, and throws some doubt on symbolism. Nevertheless, when a blockage is suspected in the unconscious, i.e., where a program is so out of date that it is blocked by new facts, dream prominence should help fashion a conclusion as to a unique trait operation. However, with the question of Q_4 as the id still "up in the air," we are sure that it rises in strength with excited and undischarged drive — hence its label "ergic tension."

[10]Throughout, we have pointed out the difference of *common* (*R, dR-*technique) and *unique* (*P*-technique) trait structures. Some psychologists may be surprised at the large role we give, in both diagnosis and treatment, to the major common traits. Much past practice — especially psychoanalytic and behavior therapy — seems to have dealt almost exclusively with what can only be called unique or compound traits. Unique attachments are, however, clearly seen — at least by psychoanalysis — as historical offshoots of drives, etc., common to everyone. We stress here that the common trait diagnosis needs to be supplemented by the common aids that therapists use to trace unique (especially unconscious) fixations; e.g., by free association, hypnosis, humor, and especially dreams. These tie the specific symptom to the measured erg, as can also be done by *P*-technique.

Incidentally, in pursuing unique attachments by dreams one must recognize that the only major alternative to Freudian interpretation of dreams is the recent "computer theory" of Evans (1983). This supposes (especially from what is known of the constructive contribution of dreams) that the REM periods in sleep are used for correction of behavioral "programs," just as computers have (nightly or periodically) to be made "off-line" as far as regular work is concerned, in order to check and tidy up the programs themselves. The theory supposes that the dream work is largely a retesting of behavioral programs against the new experiences of the dream day. There is much evidence for sleep permitting new solutions, for the REM time finishing the sorting of memories from the temporary into the long-distance memory, e.g., the much greater REM time of younger people (Evans, 1983). This does not clash with the dynamic, wish fulfillment part of Freud's theory, but still emphasizes the dream as a trial-and-error attempt at solutions.

[11]The behavioral equation uses linear and additive relations. We recognize that this involves some degree of approximation. As research proceeds, more refined curvilinear equations may be called for. But the present writer's statistical testing of some thousands of correlations has shown that only a very small minority require substitution of curvilinear forms.

If the practitioner has some clear experimental evidence of nonlinear relations he can set up, a *qualification grid* as illustrated below from data for a sales success criterion. It will be noted, for example, that success increases with increase on factor A to a sten of 8 and then declines. See Table 11.2 in the text.

Chapter 12

Some Unresolved Riddles in Structured Learning Therapy

It will be apparent that the illumination and certainty that structured learning theory brings to psychotherapy may be considered as radical as Vesalius' contribution to medicine by his introduction of studies of human anatomy, or to Rutherford's contribution to physics by discovery of the electron structure of the atom.

But, as each such discovery also exposes new questions, so structured learning theory also brings new uncertainties. This chapter is directed to that rare person: the clinician who pursues and publishes research. Two main areas call for research: (1) clarifying the meaning of the factor structure of human behavior that we presently possess, and (2) verifying the learning principles, some of which we now accept on the most slender evidence. We also need to look at relations to chemotherapy. Let us consider them in that order.

Personality structure now has over 50 years of research underlying it, based upon (a) observer ratings, (b) questionnaire and consulting-room evidence (self-exposure), and (c) objective behavioral and laboratory testing.

To those unfamiliar with the most sophisticated factor analytic and structural equation research, there seems enough disagreement to throw a fog over the *essential* agreement that exists in these fields. But even when the prevalance of mistakes in complex factorial techniques is realized and allowed for, we find most contention to be unnecessary. There is substantial agreement on 28 factors that occur consistently across domains of observation (a) and (b) in the previous paragraph — 16 in normal behavior (the 16 PF) plus 12 in abnormal behavior bring the total to 28 (the CAQ). In the newer domain of objective, behavioral tests, the O–A kit gives batteries for 10 factors and less frequently verified patterns for 10 more (Cattell and Schuerger, 1978). The factors in this objective, laboratory-measured domain show several instances (anxiety, independence, control) where they correspond to *second-order* (secondary) factors on the rating-questionnaire domain (see Chapters 3 and 4). Finally, in the last 20 years of research with *objective* motivation measures, the entire domain of some 20 ergs and at least as many sems has been mapped and measured. Alongside this broad demonstration of ability, personality, and dynamic traits, there has developed an analysis of *states*, eight dimensions measured by questionnaires and two or three (anxiety, regression, depression) measured also by objective batteries. The modulation model of states now integrates state effects with trait action in all behavioral prediction calculations by the behavioral equation.

Psychology thus has today a broad grasp of the anatomy of human behavior, concerning which we may optimistically hope that only the fringes of lesser and culturally peculiar factors remain to be filled in. The personality and ability factor patterns show constancy across several cultures (countries) and across different age groups down to about five or six years of age, giving a solid basis for developmental studies.

But with this feast of confirmed structures before us, most of them rendered available to *standardized measurement* by diligent psychometrists, we are still abysmally ignorant of what at least half the structures really mean, individually. We recognize from what Pawlik called "in-built theory," that is, the nature of the questionnaire items and the ratings, that in the rating and questionnaire media, such old clinical entities as anxiety (Q II and $U.I.$ 32), ego strength (C), superego strength (G), and several more can be reliably handled. But what is the origin (and the meaning) of factors $H, I, M,$ and Q_2, or, in the O–A kit, $U.I.$ 16, $U.I.$ 20, 21, 22, and so on?

Since the confirmation of these structures in the 1960s, clinical psychology has been astonishingly, but perhaps pardonably, slow in investigating what they are and recognizing how inevitably they will become the basis of diagnosis and prognosis. Discovery of the source *trait profiles* that define the principal DSM diagnostic groups has proceeded almost to completion. But discovery of the v weights for a variety of behaviors has been slow to the point that perhaps only half-a-dozen equations are presently known (see Cattell, Eber, and Tatsuoka, 1970). Determining b's requires more statistical expertise than psychiatrists possess, especially if one wants also the further breakdown into v's and s's. But such research should not be beyond the compass of a qualified therapist.

It is partly from the b's telling us what life behavior situations are predicted by a trait (as well as from the DSM profiles) that we gradually infer the nature of a trait. The fact that B factor in the 16 PF is high in profiles of those with good technical performance and low in profiles of mental defectives, and has large b's on verbal and mathematical ability and small ones on athletics, helps convince us, apart from its content, that it is an intelligence test. The fact that G is high in priests and low in criminals, and has high b loadings on all kinds of perseverance-demanding performances, aids its interpretation as a superego factor. We see C as ego strength partly because it has a high b on, for example, marriage adjustment, and is low in all psychopathology. And we see low O as defensiveness and high esteem because it aids quick recovery from substance abuse. The loading of I on poor recovery from neurosis, however, still does not integrate with its face meaning as "sensitivity." What, as clinicians, can we make of I factor (in 16 PF, CAQ, HSPQ, CPQ, etc.), which strongly loads neurosis (next to C) and which, in content, contains much unrealism and escape into fantasy (theatricality) along with sensitive and liberal views? It was theorized to be the product of overprotected emotional sensitivity (hence the acronym "premsia") until nature–nurture research showed it to be highly inheritable, strongly sex associated, and somewhat tied to blood group A. Some similar puzzles also exist in the *U.I.* factors in the O-A kit, despite the clarity there of extroversion, control, and anxiety.

The strategical, logical approach to theories of source traits begins by finding how much each is due respectively to *heredity* and to *learning*, and this was at last done (Cattell, 1981). We find, for example, that dominance (*E* factor) is more environmental than had been expected and that surgency–desurgency (*F* factor) is far more genetically determined. Such facts not only aid our search for source trait explanations, but also affect the therapist's plans for engendering trait change.

These accumulating findings, including the typical age growth curves, the inheritability, the change with life situation, the effect of *b*'s on life performances, and accumulating clinical experience with high and low cases, are gradually producing more complete theories about the new traits (that is, new to clinical discourse) discovered by multivariate experimental research. The results can be garnered in Cattell, Eber, and Tatsuoka (1970), Karson and O'Dell (1976), Cattell and Johnson (1986), H. Cattell (1986), and numerous articles. This dawning of meaning is particularly exciting in the case of the O-A factors, where inspection of "content" of subtests gave little information, compared to questionnaire factors. The nature and importance to the clinician of factors *U.I* 16, *U.I.* 17, *U.I.* 18, and several others has recently become particularly clear (Cattell and Schuerger, 1978).

Indeed, clinicians in general need to be reminded at this point that emerging evidence points to the O–A battery as being more powerful in diagnosis and prognosis than questionnaires or the Rorschach or any other resource they possess. This is shown in the recent work of Bjersted, Brengelman, Cattell, and Rickels, Eysenck, Killian, Knapp, Patrick, Price, Scheier, Schmidt, Schuerger, Tatro, Wardell & Yeudal, and others covered in Cattell and Schuerger's *Personality Theory in Action* (1978) and Cattell and Scheier's *Meaning and Measurement of Anxiety and Neuroticism* (1961). Thus neurotics are significantly different from controls on *U.I.* 22, cortertia (lower); *U.I.* 29, reactivity (lower); *U.I.* 16, assertiveness (lower); *U.I.* 23, regression (higher); *U.I.* 24, anxiety (higher); *U.I.* 21, exuberance (lower); and *U.I.* 28, asthenia (higher). Such a combination gives a very high degree of diagnostic separation.

Schizophrenics differ at $p < .05$ on *U.I.* 16, ego assertiveness (lower) and *U.I.* 19, independence (lower) and at $p < .001$ on lower exuberance, *U.I.* 21; greater regression, *U.I.* 23, psychotic tension, *U.I.* 25; and introversion, *U.I.* 32. Paranoid schizophrenics differ from others by being less deviant on regression, *U.I.* 32, and invia, *U.I.* 32. The O–A battery, weighted in a discriminant function, correctly placed 18 depressives and only 1 normal in the depressive category. Using only factors *U.I.* 19, 20, 25, and 30, Patrick, Cattell, et al. (1981) placed one-sixth of normals and three-quarters of diagnosed depressives in the depressive category. Similar diagnostic successes have been obtained with the O–A battery on other psychiatric DSM categories, while Cattell and Rickels (1966) have shown significant changes on the O–A battery factors with therapy. It is very evident, therefore, that the O–A source trait factors are highly relevant to clinical diagnosis; and if research clarifies further the nature of the factors, the guidance for all kinds of therapy could be very satisfactory.

In regard to factors in the 16 PF and CAQ, it is desirable that we also learn more about their mode of interaction. As far as this can be judged from their intercorrelation, we have firm knowledge thereof in the second-order factors of anxiety, exvia-invia, etc.; but there is much yet to be learned by finding how they develop these associations interactively in the life period, and how they interact in life situations. The high association of superego and self-sentiment (with some desurgency) in the restraint or control secondary Q VIII (equivalent to the O–A *U.I.* 17) almost certainly points to these all being formed simultaneously by "good upbringing" (by "middle-class morality") in the home. That the same control pattern appears in the O–A battery, in *U.I.* 17, offers one more instance of a second-order Q being a first-order T-data factor.

The associations of Q primaries in the second-order anxiety factor, Q II, are also very marked and consistent across groups and cultures. In particular, the high correlation of C − (ego weakness) with Q_4, ergic tension, is such that these factors are regularly difficult to separate by visual rotation. This surely represents what we have argued earlier: that the ego becomes strong in proportion to its success in finding outlets for frustrated ergic tension.

An interesting fact about the primary relations in the exvia-invia secondary, Q I, is that except in some child groups, dominance, E, plays no part in extraversion. The factor Q_2, self-sufficiency, has the highest loading, followed by affectia-vs.-sizia, A. Along with surgency, F, these seem to have substantial hereditary determination and support Jung's perception of extraversion as a temperament dimension. It is a reflection on the scope of the human mind that psychologists have given great attention to extraversion (exvia) and anxiety but virtually none to the equally clear peer secondaries we have just commented on, and which we call Q III (cortertia), Q IV (independence), Q V (discreetness), Q VI (prodigal subjectivity), and Q VIII (control) — all of which have clinical significance. Q III (cortertia, from "cortical alertness"), for example, is the most neurosis-associated (in the direction of being subdued), of all source traits and deserves much more intensive study. (There are indications that Q III also appears in the O–A battery as $U.I.$ 22 — loading speed of reaction, reversible perspective, etc.).

Recently, however, advance in understanding the discovered unitary traits has been reasonably rapid and is, in a sense, an inevitable consequence of clinical practice. But the second area of research defined in this chapter — that on the still uncertain principles of structured learning theory itself — is another matter. Only basic research will clarify the issues we will now discuss on influences changing personality. However, regarding therapeutic and other alleged personality changes, one has to set aside those generalizations that are merely fanciful talk. We are in a less dependable area of evidence than the multivariate experimental evidence just discussed. On experimental examination there turns out to be extremely little evidence about the effectiveness of many declared therapeutic influences, for example. One suspects, from the confused and contending literature, that a good friend often does as much good as a trained therapist immersed in theories. For example, that traits *can* be significantly altered in level by experience has only recently been shown by such data as that of Cattell, Rickels, et al. (1966) and Barton and Cattell (1972a, 1975). The former shows therapeutic change, the latter the effect of three or four years of career success, stable marriage, illness, and so forth in the ordinary life environment on such traits as dominance, superego, and surgency. The proof is, therefore, that the psychologist already has sufficiently sensitive instruments to measure significant changes, after therapy and life path experience, in meaningful variables. There is no technical excuse for continuing clinical ignorance of what can and what cannot be changed. We have the measuring instruments, and it should not be too long, therefore, before we know more about the efficacy of various therapeutic devices.

The riddle of how to change a trait level is answered in part by the New Zealand studies showing that particular life experiences over three or four years will change a specific primary trait score significantly, as shown by each particular trait measure. But though the therapist is prepared to use manipulation (e.g., by social workers) of life experience, he is rarely prepared to wait through three or four years of such manipulation. The question now needing an answer is whether anything can be done to produce significant trait change in, at most, six months of treatment.

Our earlier assumption here has been that, through knowledge of the personality structure and cognitive manipulation of the connections in the dynamic lattice, such change can be effected — at least to semic traits and some ergic tensions. As a basis for proceeding with cognitive consulting-room manipulations, we also suppose that regression therapy will first have loosened the drives we plan to reconnect to new, cognitively understood goals.

Since we hypothesize with some probability that the self-sentiment, Q_3, subsidiates, perhaps circularly, to most other sentiments and ergs, it is in the region of this sem that most cognitive reconstruction will need to be done in therapy. The patient is, say, concerned, in his self-appraisal, about his inability to get on with other people and to be popular. We ask what behaviors dictated by the self sem should be present to subsidiate to a sem of companionability and good fellowship. In such a case, one may trace obstacles in shyness, in lack of interest in others, and in lack of social and conversational skills. If these are handled as cognitive objectives, the self sem will develop a self-concept that includes them.

As mentioned earlier, there is often much to be said for initially instituting a new mode of behavior by an act of will — by the ego in the services of the self sem — and waiting for the ensuing satisfaction to make the behavior permanent *without* further aid from the will (of the ego). Generally, if the therapist explores the dynamic lattice in some later subsidiation, he will see a satisfaction unforeseen by the client, that will make the satisfaction more permanent. Action under the client's ego may also be used to detract from an undesirable course of action which subsidiated to the same goal.

Much research, requiring rather large-scale observation of everyday life, remains to be done on calculations in the dynamic lattice. We have already referred to the use of the *hydraulic principle* in understanding the changing attitude consequences of therapy, and the phenomenon of "dynamic equivalence" of symptoms. These are basically important but reasonably understood principles. What we have constantly to be aware of, however, as a new concept, is that everyone experiences changes from day to day in intentions and interests that are due to what we may call "ripple" in the dynamic lattice. Ergs differ from day to day, according to changing appetitiveness and external stimuli, as shown, for example, by Birkett and Cattell (1978) in *P*-technique; Kawash, Dielman, and Cattell (1972), Cattell, Kawash, and DeYoung (1972), and Cattell, DeYoung, Gaborit, and Barton (1973), the last on marital sex behavior. A formula underlying such change is given by:

$$E_k = b(s_k + z)[C + H + (P - G_p) + (B - G_b)] \qquad (12.1)$$

Here E_k is the ergic tension in life situation k; z is a constant to prevent E_k becoming zero when s_k is apparently zero; C is a constitutional and H an historical (Freudian) effect on the drive strength; P and B are the physiological appetitive states; and G_p and G_b are the recent alleviations (reductions, gratifications) of the regular appetitive strengths, P and B, at that time.

We have seen some developments of the dynamic lattice in Figures 9.3 and 9.4, but Figure 12.1 deals further with the combined effects of ergic change (which is due both to $b(s_k + z)$ and the appetitive terms in Equation (12.1) and to activation of sems. Only one erg (E_2) is considered to have altered, but it affects (thick lines) all of attitudes 1 through 5. Two sems, S_2 and S_3, have en-

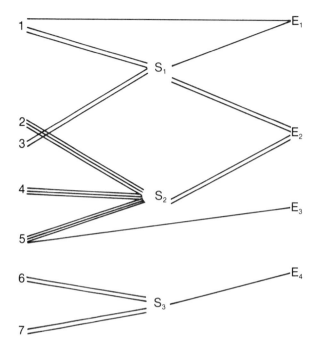

FIGURE 12.1 The "ripple" effect in the daily change in the dynamic lattice. Attitude ripple overlap of arousal of E_2 and activation of S_2 and S_3.

countered doubled cognitive stimulation, and they result in an activation increase of attitudes 2, 4, 5, 6, and 7.

It will be seen that the stimulation of one erg and two sems "ripples" through the strengths of several attitudes like criss-crossing waves in a pond. Normally in life practically all ergs and sems will be subjected to daily modulation, and we can see that the rippling of these effects across the dynamic lattice will produce a complex multiple interaction resulting in changing strengths on virtually all attitudes. These origins of change in attitudes can nevertheless, in principle, be sorted out by *P*- or *R*-technique (principally the former) because most experiences will be unique to a person. The formula for any one attitude, *j*, remains the same as before:

$$a_{hijk} = \Sigma v_{jg} s_{kg} E_g + \Sigma v_{je} s_{ke} E_e + \Sigma v_{jme} s_{km} ME$$

$$+ \Sigma v_{jem} s_{ke} EM + \Sigma v_{jm} s_{km} M \qquad (12.2)$$

where s_{kg} is the innate part of the stimulation from k and s_{ke} is the environmentally acquired part; s_{km} is the activation given to the sem, and s_{ke} is that given to the erg. The Σ signs remind us that this occurs over all ergs and sems in the lattice. Equation (12.2) expresses the result in any particular attitude, and by working it out for all attitudes we can express the ripple effect in attitudes from moment to moment. Our finding, for example, that the total fluctuation in attitudes over a few days is inversely related to ego strength shows that the ego is in some way a dampener of rippling. This is probably because the ego recognizes some of the external stimulation of ergs and sems as being undesirable, and some of the appetitive stimulation of ergs as being in need of control, to prevent the disturbance from extending so readily to the attitudes. Thus research needs to consider the role of the control system — notably C, G, and Q_3 — as it interferes with the normal ripple effect. There may also be inherent laws to be discovered in the ripple interaction. For these, changes in the intensity of attitudes explain what people spontaneously do in the course of everyday life.

While this daily change is of considerable therapeutic interest and importance, we must for the present leave it as an only partially understood mystery of everyday sequences and turn to more immediate research needs. Let us consider again the important sem we call the self-sentiment (Q_3 in CAQ and SS in the MAT). Since we conclude that it subsidiates to most other sentiments and ergs, it is in the region of this sem that most cognitive reconstruction will need to be done. The patient is, say, concerned about his inability to get on with other people and to be popular. What behaviors dictated by the self sem should be present to subsidiate to a sem of companionability and good fellowship? In such a case one may trace obstacles in shyness, in lack of interest in others, and in lack of social and conversational skills. If these are handled as cognitive objects, the self sem will develop a self-concept that includes them. As mentioned earlier, there is often much to be said for initially instituting a new mode of behavior by an act of will — by the ego in the service of the self sem — and waiting for the ensuing satisfaction to become permanent *without* aid from the will of the ego. Generally, if the therapist explores the dynamic lattice, he will see a satisfaction on some later subsidiation, unforeseen by the client, that will make the satisfaction more permanent. Action dictated by the client's ego may also be used to detract from an undesirable course of action that originally subsidiated to the same goal. Thus, in one case, exciting reading was put in the hands of an adolescent with an almost obsessive interest in movies. It is true that the deeper problem of a fantasy escape from an unhappy home life existed in this case, but the substitute satisfaction at least balanced a life style while detachment from the home was being managed.

One sees here the alteration of a b value in the process of building up a trait. The alteration of b values is largely through CR I and CR II (Table 11.3 in the previous chapter) but principally the latter: *means–end learning*. It is simple to show, cognitively, to what firm preexisting sentiment (shown to be strong by the MAT) a new course of behavior will serve. A woman's self-sentiment about her figure often produces a dietary change. But these internal rewards can be planned only with a knowledge of what factors are large on the MAT and what the subsidiations are in the dynamic lattice. This is a central gain from using the viewpoint of structured learning theory. We have assumed (in the absence of P-technique) that the therapist's concepts of the form of the patient's dynamic lattice, as stated above, will be formed by conversation, and, where unconscious breaks occur in the lattice, by the methods known since Freud. However, it is possible that advances in structured learning theory may put more economical methods into our hands.

Beyond these practical steps that need to be experimentally tested and put into action, on the basis of present structured learning theory, there remain, as this chapter heading indicates, mysteries to be solved in basic structured learning itself. Since these may go beyond the immediate interests of clinicians, we shall state the needed research with extreme brevity, but clearly enough to benefit the researcher who will continue to read on. However, before entering that realm, we have to clarify a matter of importance to the practitioner, namely, the use of medication.

Freud early recognized that schizophrenia was beyond his positive treatment. The study of Kallman (1953) and more controlled
studies since (see Cattell, 1981, Chapter 2) show about 70 percent
of identical twins of schizophrenics also to be schizophrenic, and
about 60 percent of children to be schizophrenics when both parents
are schizophrenic. The proportions for manic-depressive inheritance
are, if anything, somewhat higher. These facts, together with the
discoveries of abnormal brain function, in hormones, etc., justify
our treating psychosis as totally different from neurosis. Some forms
of chemotherapy, e.g., chlorpromazine in schizophrenics and Lithium in manic depressives, have been so successful as to suggest that
soon chemotherapy will be the main treatment, with psychotherapy as only a "tidying" adjustment process.

However, depression and anxiety are also common symptoms
in neurosis, and the alternative presents itself of treating them with
drugs, e.g., Imipramine and Valium, respectively. The psychotherapist is apt to regard the free use of these drugs as a temporary and
questionable aid. If the persisting physiological proneness component of anxiety in anxiety hysteria is relieved by drugs such as
Valium, must the dose be continued throughout the patient's life,
or does some "learning to live without anxiety" occur, so that dosages
may be reduced? We do not today have any positive experimental
answer, but from what we know of biofeedback treatments it seems
possible that the experience of reward in reduced anxiety may lead
to the drug experience lasting to some degree after its withdrawal.

Although both anxiety and depression tend to reduce several cognitive performances, e.g., memory, low degrees of anxiety can operate to produce learning, as shown by Spence and others, though
all higher values are negatively associated with cognitive learning
(Spielberger, 1972; Cattell & Scheier, 1961). The question about
drug use that the therapist may ask is whether the reduction of anxiety (and also depression) by drugs causes loss of some of the drive
(and plasticity of effort in the case of depression) needed to produce psychic learning. Boyle (1984), for example, shows anxiety
(as a state) to be slightly positively correlated to the acquisition of
superego strength, but also correlated to the generation of pugnaci-

ty. We know that, in the long run (Horn, 1961; Gorsuch, 1965), superego strength becomes, *in normal subjects, negatively* related to anxiety (unlike Freud's neurotic subjects). Anxiety can be considered a storage of frustrated drive and may be, in many circumstances, a driving force for superego growth (and also ergic reconstruction). The use of drugs to change moods therefore has to be considered, in structured learning, with strategic insight, not only as a temporary prop in the case, for example, of suicidal depression.

Let us now summarize the structured learning issues needing experimental investigation.

1. Enrichment of meaning and measurements is needed by finding fresh objective tests to measure the U and I motivation components, and to clarify the third, still shadowy factor found in the work of Sweney, Radcliffe, McGraw, and Anton. Do the U and I components change in mutual level with time, therapy, and life experience? Does the $(U\text{-}I)$ conflict measure agree with other conflict measures, notably those of Cattell and Sweney (1964)? Do the primary components express products of or additions to the motivation and the device endowment? An improvement in the sensitivity of objective motivation measurement devices is a scientific advance devoutly to be wished, for all kinds of diagnosis, monitoring, and research on situational influences demand equal validity with much shorter time than many devices now take. Possibly EEG and EKG research will yield such "quick" devices, valid against the longer devices now used in the MAT, etc.

2. What ergs and sems remain to be discovered by new samples of attitudes? Can one detect any ergic bonding formations corresponding to Jung's archetypes?

3. Will factoring at various childhood levels reveal growth in organization of sem fragments as indicated by Sweeney and Cattell (1964)? And can more cogent data be found relating sem growth to our three principles of (a) common reinforcement, (b) agency action, and (c) budding? This could be checked by animal experiment, controlling the stimuli (Cattell and Dielman, 1974).

4. More experiments are needed, on the lines of Fleishman's

(1967) and Hendrick's (1971), to demonstrate that life and learning produce systematic changes in the ergic and semic *investment* loadings in an attitude over time.

5. Can the distinction of *arousal* of an erg and *activation* of a sem be consolidated by state experiment measures and brain physiology? And does the activation of a sem operate as a cognitive network, able to be stimulated *as a whole* by stimulators of *any* attitude parts? Unity of change has been shown by *dR*-technique; but is what produces the change an appetitive change on a set of constituent ergs, or a cognitive stimulus of sem network associations?

6. Similarly, can the ergic tension equation be checked as to the relations of s_k, H, and the appetitive terms as presently hypothesized? The experiments of Adelson (1952), DeYoung, Cattell, Gaborit, and Barton (1973) show the effects of s_k and appetitiveness to be as supposed, but presently support nothing more precise.

7. Are the reciprocal concepts of *ergic investment of a sem* and of *sem mandates of an erg* calculable as now defined, and do they have the expected relations to other terms, such as magnitude of anger and depression, on their frustration?

8. Do experiments on blocking a particular path in the dynamic lattice lead to theorized consequences in (a) changes in strength of other paths, (b) state changes in anger, anxiety, and depression, and (c) breadth of relearning in proportion to depression engendered?

9. Can a single factor of total personality integration, such as C factor, be demonstrated among measures of (a) total indurated conflict, as $\Sigma\overline{b}$ in William's (1959) experiment, (b) the Cattell-Sweney conflict (1974) measures, (c) instability of attitudes by test–retest, (d) cognitive dissonance by Cattell's "logical inconsistency" measure, (1943) and (e) correlation of the Birkett measures of panels of ego (C) action strength (Cattell and Birkett, 1980b)?

10. Does decision theory, in *active conflict* situations, work as expected? That is, can one, from knowledge of a person's E and M scores, and of the b's for two courses of action, predict what the person's decision will be? [The preliminary experiments of Laughlin (1972) were inconclusive beyond the $p < .05$ level).

11. Can the theory that a sem defines a *procedure* as well as a *struc-*

ture be verified by observations of humans or lower animals? That is to say, is action toward a goal directed by a combination of stimuli and needs, standing at given values, as hypothesized in the bottom of the "ripple" diagram (p. 153)?

12. Is the reward in learning fixed by the decline at the goal of *need* strength, or of the *arousal* level, or both? And does the linear decline of cognitive reverberation of an intermediate action cognitively, explain the amount of engramming, as given in the formula (12.1)?

13. Learning can be predicted in part, we know from Cattell and Butcher (1968), from the *extant* stable levels of dynamic traits, but presumably more completely when the rewards are also taken into account. The rewards to ergs can be taken simply as a drop in tension level; but those to sems could depend on what part of ergic investment in a sem is rewarded. For example, the sentiment to home might be rewarded in saving money to send home; but it would be mainly the succoring, parental protective erg in the sem that would be rewarded by that action. Accordingly, each sem term in the reward needs to be multiplied by a fraction representing only the specific invested ergs in the sem. This fraction would vary in magnitude with the particular attitude, as shown by the v terms in the following: learning in attitude xki:

$$l_{xki} = v_{xy}s_{ky}(E_{y1i} - E_{y2i}) + v_{xz}s_{kz}f_{zx}(M_{1i} - M_{2i}) \qquad (12.3)$$

where the subscripts are as usual (p. 3); the reward between beginning and ending of the learning is $(E_{y1i} - E_{y2i})$ and $f_{2x}(M_{1i} - M_{2i})$, f_{zx} being the fraction of the ergic investment that bears on learning l_x in situation k.

14. We need investigation in full detail of two or three normal dynamic lattices, simultaneously by factor analysis, by blocking experiments, and, of course, by questioning and free association, to discover the typical complexities of subsidiation among sems: in particular, to confirm the position of the self-sentiment as most distal from the ergic goals. The cumulative evidence of manipulation of ergs and sems by stimuli (Cattell, Kawash, and DeYong, 1972; Cattel and Brennan, 1986; Boyle and Cattell, 1984) is that production of change in ergic arousal is more significant than in sem activation, and that in ergs the larger change is in the U than in the I component. One might expect the latter if it takes time for a basic U change to be converted into new cognition (I factor) outlets. The plotting of lattice changes therefore needs to be followed separately in U and I component measures.

15. To examine the soundness of operational measures of the concept of *deflection strain*. This concerns measures of the "distance" of acquired paths to ergic goals from a determinable "innately most natural path." Deflection strain, determined for a whole cultural group, is theorized to have much importance for social-psychological problems, in particular as a measure of the cultural pressure factor in revolutions. The distance might be measured by observations of frequency of regressions, as well as by comparison of the b's for a particular erg in

$$a_{hijk} = b_{hjk1}E_{1i} + b_{hjk2}E_{2i} \qquad (12.4)$$

where the first b is the amount of reaction to hjk from an innate connection and the second b the acquired contribution to the response a_{hijk}. E_1 and E_2 could be the same, if we imagine the differentiation to occur purely through the v values.

This listing of fifteen main issues in structured learning and the dynamic calculus points to the most important solutions or confirmations needed if therapeutic practice is to be put on a more effective scientific footing. They are listed here for basic interest and the guidance of student and professional research. A somewhat fuller discussion, with definite designs for experiment, are given elsewhere (Cattell, 1976, 1980a).

Looking at these proposals, one is compelled to recognize that the average reader, having his head filled with the particularities of reflexological theory and the more superficial fads of the practitioner's marketplace, will have difficulties. He will experience, perhaps, the same sense of unreality as did psychologists at the beginning of the century in understanding Freud. In the first place, although these proposals are based on concrete measurement, they express themselves in precise psychometric formulae, of which most clinicians are said to be terrified. One reaction to this shock — e.g., in Eysenck's (1982) approach to structured learning — has simply been to deny the support of a concrete data base for structured learning formulae. This is possible only by the deliberate cultivation of ignorance of the voluminous literature in this field, which a fair number of the current generation and their students have already actually accomplished. It involves, for example, denial of "trait theories" so-called, i.e., denial that objects have their characteristics. (See note 12 in Chapter 11.) It involves quibbling about linear relations. It involves blowing up minor disagreements among amateur factor analysts as if they were disagreements of experts. It involves refusing to become familiar with and to learn the wealth of new trait structures laid out in the last fifty years of replicated research. It involves failing to understand the meaning and integrations of *R*-, *P*-, and *dR*-techniques in state, situation, and trait interaction. Finally, it requires that the misguided psychologist belittle any diagnosis by sophisticated instruments.

In this connection, the present writer was asked by one editor to add here a large section to familiarize what he considered a majority of readers with the broad array of traits and research foundations on structured personality. I could only ask, "Where have these students of personality been in the last fifty years?" I declined because the foundations and methods have already been set out in almost countless publications. Among these I would call attention particularly to Cattell and Warburton (1967), Cattell and Scheier (1961), Eysenck (1967), Pervin (1970), Cartwright (1970), Hall and Lindzey (1957), Smith and Vetter (1982), and my own *Personality* (1950), *Abilities, Their Structure, Growth and Action* (1961), *Personality and Mood by Questionnaire* (1973b), *Motivation Structure* (with Child, 1975), *Handbook of Modern Personality Theory* (with Dreger, 1977), *Personality and Learning Theory* (1979), and *Functional Psychological Testing* (with Johnson, 1986). These will enlarge on the experimental bases of various statements made rather briefly about the applied field in this book.

The points in this book at which operational, experimental evidence ends and sheer theoretical propositions begin will be clear to most readers. The trait and state structures, their correlations with life criteria, and their changes under situations are more replicated in research than some critics evidently realize. The formulae for decision, conflict, and learning only recently have support emerging. But they are all available for experiment, since tolerable measuring instruments now are available, e.g., on the activation of sems as *unitary* networks, and answers are emerging in the most recent publications. These formulae are somewhat simpler than what one perceives as being faithful to nature, but I have felt it undesirable to overburden the applied reader in his first struggles with a new domain. The bases for unitary functional measurement, in the 16 PF, CAQ, CAB, MAT, SMAT, HSPQ, the 8-State Measures, and even the Humor and Musical Choice Tests, are now available and standardized to make such research possible. It is true that the newest structural research has so far succeeded only in marking out and holding the factor structure by stated patterns in a domain; and even more established, standardized scales are admittedly in need of "progressive rectification" for greater validity. These latter corrections, however, are by straightforward (largely "itemetric") procedures that the larger circle of laboratories with minimal technical resources can tackle.

What is in doubt revolves around changes in the social history of psychology as a science, as it approaches the status of psychonomy. For altogether too long clinicians have taken refuge in therapy "as an art" and have used inefficient diagnostic methods like Rorschach, "drawing a man," the five-factor MMPI, the three-factor EPI, and various concoctions of practice that are paralleled in rationale and efficiency by seventeenth-century medicine. A new day is dawning, and new, more effective complexities are being understood. Many today correctly perceive the closing years of the twentieth century as the time of a true revolution in psychological theory and practice. We are moving toward more complete and penetrating psychometry and the development of theory that will stand up under computation. In psychology itself we can hope to see a comparative reduction in the use of the less effective bivariate designs (oddly still called "experimental psychology") and the growth of sophisticated multivariate experiment, via factor analysis and the fitting of structural equations. We have puttered too long with near-surface and qualitative guesses, when the important relations and laws are likely to be found in calculations at higher and deeper levels, among measures of ergic tensions, conflict, integration, and structured learning findings. This will come when psychology students reach the level of those in, say, engineering, chemistry, and medicine. Then computer-aided diagnosis and the monitoring of therapy in its complex longitudinal processes will at last become everyday procedures.

One cannot but be a little jealous of the wonder that these therapists of the future will experience and at the possibilities of control they will possess. Let us hope that this book will be a start in that direction, though it may be for some a difficult start.

Finally, as we obtain more power over our medium, it is not inappropriate to end with a note on what functional diagnoses and structured learning theory mean for the *ethics* of practice. Does any person have the right — which practitioners assume — to alter another person's personality? This was questioned by, for example, Bernard Shaw, in the parallel case of education, and some question it in therapy — even with the full consent of the patient. Earlier we have asked, "What is the definition of the healthy personality, toward which the therapist leads his patient?" We have answered that *for a given society* the profile that we call healthy can be defined in measurements. Indeed, only the fact that a standard of freedom from mental illness can be stated in an objective profile leaves the ethics of patient manipulation free from the subjectivity of the practitioner. Thus a more overt and objective scientific basis is also the beginning of evaluating the ethics of practice.

References

Adelson, M. (1952) *A Study of Ergic Tension Pattern Affects Through the Deprivation of Water in Humans.* Unpublished Ph.D. thesis, University of Illinois, Urbana.

Bandura, A. (1962) Social learning through imitation. In Jones, M. R. (ed.), *Nebraska symposium on motivation.* Lincoln: University of Nebraska Press.

Barton, K., and Cattell, R. B. (1972a) Personality before and after a chronic illness. *Journal of Clinical Psychology 28*: 466–467.

Barton, K., and Cattell, R. B. (1972b) Personality factors in relation to job turnover and promotion. *Journal of Counselling Psychology 19*: 430–435.

Barton, K., and Cattell, R. B. (1975) Changes in personality over a 5-year period; relationship of changes to life events. JSAS *Catalogue of Selected Documents in Psychology.*

Birkett, H., and Cattell, R. B. (1978) Diagnosis of the dynamic roots of a clinical symptom by P-technique: A case of episodic alcoholism. *Multivariate Experimental Clinical Research 3*: 173–194.

Bleuler, M. (1933) The definition of influences of environment and heredity on mental disposition. *Character and Personality 1*: 286–300.

Boyle, G. J. (1983a) Effects on academic learning of manipulating emotional states and motivation dynamics. *British Journal of Educational Psychology 53*: 347–357.

Boyle, G. J. (1983b) High order factor structure of Cattell's MAT and 8SQ. *Multivariate Experimental Clinical Research 6*: 119–127.

Boyle, G. J. (1984) Effects of viewing a road trauma film on emotional and motivational factors. *Individual Differences and Personality 4:* 1–7.

Boyle, G. J. (1985) Unintegrated and integrated dynamics in the motivation analysis test (MAT); evidence of their state and trait nature. *Educational and Psychological Measurement.*

Boyle, G. J., and Cattell, R. B. (1984) Proof of situational sensitivity of mood states and dynamic traits. *Individual Psychology* (1986).

Boyle, Y. G. (1985) Superfactors in Cattell's 16PF, Eight State Battery and Objective Motivational Analysis Battery (MA). *Australian Journal of Psychology 41*: 10–20.

Brunswick, E. (1956) *Perception and the representative design of psychological experiments*. Berkeley: University of California Press.

Burt, C. L. (1927) *The young delinquent*. London: University of London Press.

Cartwright, D. W. (1974) *Introduction to personality theory*. Englewood Cliffs, N.J.: Prentice-Hall.

Cattell, H. (1984) *The art of combining tests, biography and interview in psychotherapy*.

Cattell, H. (1985) The art of clinical assessment by the 16PF, CAQ and MAT. In Cattell, R. B., and Johnson, R. B., *Functional psychological testing*. New York: Brunner Mazel.

Cattell, R. B. (1943) Fluctuation of sentiment and attitudes as a measure of character integration and temperament. *American Journal of Psychology 56*: 195–216.

Cattell, R. B. (1953) On the theory of group learning. *Journal of Social Psychology 17*: 27–52.

Cattell, R. B. (1960) The dimensional measurement of anxiety, excitement, effort states and other mood reaction batteries. In Uhr, L., and Miller, J. G. (eds.), *Drugs and behavior*. New York: Wiley.

Cattell, R. B. (1963) Formulating the environmental situation and its perception, in behavior theory. In Sells, S. B. (ed.), *Stimulus determinants of behavior*. New York: Ronald Press.

Cattell, R. B. (1964) The parental early repressiveness hypothesis for the authoritarian personality factor U.I.28. *Journal of Genetic Psychology 106*: 332–349.

Cattell, R. B. (1970) *The culture fair intelligence tests, scales I, II and III*. Champaign, IL: IPAT.

Cattell, R. B. (1973a) The interpretation of Pavlov's typology and the arousal concept in replicated trait and state factors. In Gray, J. A. (ed.), *Biological bases of individual behavior*. New York: Academic Press.

Cattell, R. B. (1973b) *Personality and mood by questionnaire*. San Francisco: Jossey Bass.

Cattell, R. B. (1973c) The measurement of the healthy personality and the healthy society. *The Counselling Psychologist 4*: 13–18.

Cattell, R. B. (1974) How good is the modern questionnaire: General principles for evaluation. *Journal of Personality Assessment 38*: 115–129.

Cattell, R. B. (1975) *The motivation analysis test*. Champaign, IL: IPAT.

Cattell, R. B. (1976) *Great experiments in dynamic psychology — not yet done*. Champaign, IL: IPAT.

Cattell, R. B. (1978) *The scientific use of factor analysis.* New York: Praeger.

Cattell, R. B. (1979) *Personality and learning theory I. The structure of personality in its environment.* New York: Springer Publishing Co.

Cattell, R. B. (1980a) *Personality and learning theory II. A systems theory of motivation and structured learning.* New York: Springer Publishing Co.

Cattell, R. B. (1980b) The structured learning analysis of therapeutic change and maintenance. In Karoly, B., and Steffens, J. J. (eds.), *Improving the long term effects of therapy.* New York: Gardner.

Cattell, R. B. (1981) *The inheritance of personality and ability.* New York: Academic Press.

Cattell, R. B. (1985) *Human motivation and the dynamic calculus.* New York: Praeger.

Cattell, R. B., Barton, K., and Vaughan, D. (1973) Changes in personality as a function of college attendance and work experience. *Journal of Counselling Psychology 20*: 162–165.

Cattell, R. B., and Birkett, H. (1980a) Can P-technique diagnosis be practically shortened? *Multivariate Experimental Clinical Research 5*: 1–16.

Cattell, R. B., and Birkett, H. (1980b) The known personality factors found aligned between first order T-data and second order Q-data factors, with new evidence on inhibitory control. *Personality and Individual Differences 1*: 229–238.

Cattell, R. B., and Bjersted, A. (1967) The structure of depression by factoring Q-data in relation to general personality source traits. *Scandinavian Journal of Psychology 8*: 17–24.

Cattell, R. B., and Brennan, J. (1983) The cultural types of modern nations by two quantitative classification methods. *Sociology and Social Research 68*: 208–233.

Cattell, R. B., and Brennan, J. (1985) Intelligence factors g_f and g_c in the elderly. *Journal of Applied Developmental Psychology 20*: 1–17.

Cattell, R. B., and Brennan, J. (1986) State measurement: a check on the fit of the modulation model to anxiety and depression states. *Journal of Mathematical Psychology* (in press).

Cattell, R. B., Brennan, J., Rao, C., and Kameoka, V. (1984) The heritability of the clinically relevant personality factors guilt proneness (O), parmia (H), and ergic tension (Q_4) by MAVA and the maximum likelihood methods. *Japanese Journal of Psychology 25*, 9–21.

Cattell, R. B., and Butcher, J. (1968) *The prediction of achievement and creativity.* Indianapolis: Bobbs Merrill.

Cattell, R. B., Cattell, A. K., and Rhymer, R. M. (1947) P-technique demonstrated in determining psycho-physiological source traits in a normal individual. *Psychometrika 12*: 267–288.

Cattell, R. B., and Child, D. (1975) *Motivation and dynamic structures.* Champaign, IL: IPAT.

Cattell, R. B., Coulter, M. A., and Tsujioka, B. (1966) The taxonometric recognition of types and functional emergents. In Cattell, R. B. (ed.), *Handbook of multivariate experimental psychology*. Chicago: Rand McNally, pp. 288–329.

Cattell, R. B., DeYoung, G. E., and Barton, K. A. (1978) A check in the validity of motivation measurement of the hunger erg. *British Journal of Psychology 71*: 10–25.

Cattell, R. B., and Dielman, T. E. (1974) The structure of motivation manifestations as measured in the laboratory rat: An examination of motivation and component theory. *Social Behavior and Personality 2*: 10–24.

Cattell, R. B., Dielman, T. E., and Barton, K. (1973) Cross validational evidence on the structure of parental reports of child rearing practices. *Journal of Social Psychology 90*: 243–250.

Cattell, R. B., Dielman, T. E., and Barton, K. (1974) Child rearing practices and achievement in school. *Journal of Genetic Psychology 24*: 155–165.

Cattell, R. B., Eber, H. J., and Tatsuoka, M. (1970) *Handbook for the sixteen personality factor questionnaire*. Champaign, IL: IPAT.

Cattell, R. B., Horn, J. L., Radcliffe, J., and Sweney, A. B. (1963) The nature and measurement of components of motivation. *Genetic Psychology Monographs 68*: 49–218.

Cattell, R. B., and Johnson, R. C. (1986) *Functional psychological testing*. New York: Brunner Mazel.

Cattell, R. B., and Kameoka, V. A. (1985) Psychological states measured in the Clinical Analysis Questionnaire (CAQ). *Multivariate Experimental Clinical Research 7*: 69–87.

Cattell, R. B., Kawash, G. F., and DeYoung, G. E. (1972) Validation of objective measures of ergic tensions: Response of the sex erg to visual stimulation. *Journal of Experimental Research on Personality 6*: 76–83.

Cattell, R. B., Rickels, K., Weise, C., Gray, B., and Yee, R. (1966) The effects of psychotherapy upon anxiety (U.I.24) and regression (U.I.23). *American Journal of Psychotherapy 20*: 261–269.

Cattell, R. B., and Scheier, J. H. (1961) *The Meaning and Measurement of Anxiety and Neuroticism*. New York: Ronald Press.

Cattell, R. B., and Schuerger, J. M. (1978) *Personality theory in action*. Champaign, Ill.: IPAT.

Cattell, R. B., and Sweney, A. B. (1964) Components measurable in manifestations of mental conflict. *Journal of Abnormal and Social Psychology 68*: 479–490.

Cattell, R. B., and Tatro, D. F. (1966) The personality traits, objectively measured, that distinguish psychotics from normals. *Behaviour Research and Therapy 4*: 39–57.

Cattell, R. B., and Warburton, F. W. (1967) *Objective personality and motivation tests: A theoretical introduction and practical compendium.* Champaign, Ill.: University of Illinois Press.

Cattell, R. B., and Wenig, P. (1952) Dynamic and cognitive factors controlling misperception. *Journal of Abnormal and Social Psychology 47*: 797–809.

Cagley, J. M., and Savage, R. D. (1984) Differences of stressed and unstressed military veterans. *Australian Journal of Psychology 20:* $120–130.

Clore, G. L., and Byrne, D. (1977) The process of personality interaction. In Cattell, R. B., and Dreger, R. M. (eds.), *Handbook of modern personality theory.* Washington, D.C.: Hemisphere Books, Chapter 22.

Curran, J. P., and Cattell, R. B. (1976) *Handbook for the 8-state battery.* Champaign, Ill.: IPAT.

DeYoung, G. E., Cattell, R. B., Gaborit, M., and Barton, E. G. (1973) A causal model of the effects of personality and marital role factors upon diary reported sexual behavior. *Proceedings of the 81st Annual Convention of the APA*, Montreal, Canada, *8*: 357–358.

Ellis, H. C., and Hunt, R. R. (1972) *Fundamentals of human memory and cognition.* Dubuque, IA: Brown.

Evans, D. (1983) *The nature of dreams.* New York: Wiley.

Eysenck, H. J. (1967) *The biological basis of personality.* Springfield, IL: Thomas.

Eysenck, H. J. (1982) Review of Cattell's *Personality and Learning Theory. Personality and Individual Differences 3*: 1–4.

Eysenck, H. J., and Rachman, E. (1965) *The causes and cures of neurosis: An introduction to modern behavior therapy.* San Diego: Knapp, 1965.

Fleishman, E. A. (1967) Development of a behavioral taxonomy for describing human tasks: A correlational-experimental approach. *Journal of Applied Psychology 51*: 1–10.

Fleishman, E. O. (1967) Individual differences in motor learning, In R. M. Gagne (Ed.). *Learning and individual differences.* Columbus: Bobbs Merrill.

Freud, A. (1937) *The ego and the mechanisms of defense.* London: Hogarth.

Freud, S. (1949) *Outline of psychoanalysis.* New York: Norton.

Frey, D., and Carlock, C. J. (1984) *Enhancing self esteem.* Muncie, IN: Accelerated Development.

Fromm, E. (1973) *The anatomy of human destructiveness.* New York: Holt, Rinehart, & Winston.

Gorsuch, R. L. (1965) *The clarification of some factors in the area of super-ego behavior.* Unpublished master's thesis, University of Illinois, Urbana, IL.

Hakstian, R. (1976) *The comprehensive ability test (CAB).* Champaign, IL: IPAT.

Hakstian, A. R., and Cattell, R. B. (1976) *The comprehensive ability battery (CAB)*. Champaign, Ill.: IPAT.

Hall, C. S., and Lindzey, G. (1957) *Theories of personality*. New York: Wiley.

Hendricks, B. C. (1971) *The Sensitivity of the Dynamic Calculus to Short Term Change in Interest Structure*. Unpublished M.A. thesis, University of Illinois, Urbana.

Hernon, W. W., and Iverson, I. H. (1970) *Classical conditioning and operant conditioning: A response pattern analysis*. New York: Springer Publishing Co.

Hom, J. L. (1961) *Structure in measures of self sentiment, ego and superego concepts*. Unpublished master's thesis, University of Illinois, Urbana, IL.

Horn, J. L. (1972) State, trait and change dimensions of intelligence. *British Journal of Educational Psychology 42*: 159–185.

Horn, J. L., and Sweney, A. B. (1968) The dynamic calculus model for motivation and its use in understanding the individual case. In Mahrer, A. R. (ed.), *New approaches to psychodiagnostic systems*. New York: Wiley.

Hundleby, J. D. (1968) The trait of anxiety, as defined by objective performances and indices of emotional disturbance, in middle childhood. *Multivariate Behavioral Research*, Special Issue, 7–14.

Izard, C. E. (1971) *The face of emotion*. New York: Appleton-Century-Crofts.

James, G., and Lott, A. G. (1964) Reward frequency and the formulation of positive attitudes toward group members. *Journal of Social Psychology 62*: 111–115.

Jensen, A. R. (1962) Extroversion, neuroticism and serial learning. *Psychologua 20*: 66–67.

Jordan, T. E. (1971) Early developmental adversity and the first two years of life. *Multivariate Behavioral Research Monographs 3*: 61–81.

Jung, C. G. (1953) *Two essays on analytical psychology*. New York: Pantheon.

Kallman, T. J. (1953) *Heredity in health & mental disorders*. New York: Norton.

Kameoka, V. (1986) The structure of the Clinical Analysis Questionnaire and depression symptomatology. *Multivariate Behavioral Research, 21*, 105–122.

Kamfer, F. H., and Marsten, C. R. (1963) Determinants of self-reinforcement in human learning. *Journal of Experimental Psychology 58*: 245–254.

Karson, S., and O'Dell, M. (1976) *The clinical use of the 16 PF*. Champaign, IL: Institute for Personality and Ability Testing.

Kawash, G. W., Dielman, T. E., and Cattell, R. B. (1972) Changes in objective measures of fear motivation as a function of laboratory controlled manipulation. *Psychological Reports 30*: 59–63.

Kesson, S. (1965) Primary factor correlations of boys with personality and conduct problems. *Journal of Clinical Psychology 21*: 16–18.

Knapp, R. R. (1963) Personality correlates of delinquency rates in a Navy sample. *Journal of Applied Psychology 47*: 68–71.

Kohlberg, L. (1973) Moralization: The cognitive developmental approach. In Baltes, P. B., and Schaie, K. W. (eds.), *Life span developmental psychology*. New York: Academic Press.

Krasner, L., and Ullman, L. P. (1965) *Research in behavior modification*. New York: Holt, Rinehart & Winston.

Kretschmer, C. (1925) *Korperbau und Charakter*. New York: Harcourt Brace.

Krug, S. E. (1977a) An experimental alteration of motivation levels in adolescents. *Multivariate Experimental Clinical Research 3*: 43–51.

Krug, S. E. (1977b) *Personality assessment in psychological medicine*. Champaign, IL: IPAT.

Krug, S. E., and Cattell, R. B. (1971) A test of the "trait view" theory of distortion in measurement of personality by questionnaire. *Educational and Psychological Measurement 31*: 721–734.

Krug, S. E., & Laughlin, J. (1976) Handbook for the IPAT depression scale. Champaign, IL: IPAT.

Landes, J. T. (1960) The trauma of children when parents divorce. *Marriage and Family Living 26*: 7–13.

Laughlin, J. (1972) Prediction of action decisions from the dynamic calculus. Master's thesis. University of Illinois, Urbana, Ill.

Lazarus, P. (1966) *Psychological stress and the coping process*. New York: McGraw Hill.

Lazarus, R. S., Deese, J., and Hamilton, R. (1952) Anxiety and stress in learning. *Journal of Experimental Psychology 47*: 111–114.

Leontieff, B. (1966) The nature of conditioning. Presidential address, 21st International Congress of Psychology, Moscow.

Lidz, R. W., and Lidz, T. (1949) The family environment of schizophrenic patients. *Journal of American Psychiatry 106*: 332–345.

Lorr, M., and Klett, C. J. (1969) Cross cultural comparison of psychotic syndromes. *Journal of Abnormal Psychology 74*: 531–542.

Lorr, M., O'Connor, J. P., and Stafford, J. (1957) Confirmation of nine psychotic syndrome patterns. *Journal of Clinical Psychology 13*: 252–257.

Luborsky, J., and Mintz, J. (1972) The contributions of P-technique to personality, psychotherapy and psychosomatic research. In Dreger, R. M. (ed.), *Contribution to the study of personality in honor of Raymond B. Cattell*. Baton Rouge, LA: Claitor.

Lynn, R. (1966) *Attention, arousal and the orientation reactions*. Oxford, England: Pergamon.

Lytton, H. (1971) Observational studies of parent-child interaction: A methodological review. *Child Development 42*: 651–684.

Madsen, K. B. (1974) *Theories of motivation*. New York: Wiley.

Malmo, R. B. (1959) Activation: A neuro-psychological dimension. *Psychological Review 66*: 367–386.

Marston, A. R. (1965) Imitation, self reinforcement and reinforcement of another person. *Journal of Personality and Social Psychology 2*: 255–261.

McArdle, J. (1985) Structural equation modelling of an individual system: preliminary results from a case of episodic alcoholism (in press). *Multivariate Experimental Clinical Research.*

McDougall, W. (1932). *The energies of man*. London: Methuen.

Mefferd, R. B. (1966) Structured physiological correlates of mental processes and states. In Cattell, R. B. (ed.), *Handbook of multivariate experimental psychology*. Chicago: Rand McNally.

Mehlman, B. (1952) The reliability of psychiatric diagnosis. *Journal of Abnormal and Social Psychology 47*: 577–587.

Meredith, G. M. (1967) Observations of the origin and current status of the ego assertive personality factor, U.I.16. *Journal of Genetic Psychology 110*: 269–286.

Moss, H. G., and Kagan, J. (1964) Report on personality consistency and change from the Tels longitudinal study. *Vita Humana 7*: 127–138.

The Motivational Analysis Test (MAT). (1959) Champaign, Ill.: IPAT.

Mowrer, O. H., and Allman, A. D. (1985) Time as a determinant in integrative learning. *Psychological Review 52*: 61–90.

Muhl, P. I. (1950) On the circularity of the law of effect. *Psychological Bulletin 47*: 52–57.

Nesselroade, J. R., and Ford, D. H. (1985) *P*-technique comes of age. *Research on Aging, 1.*

Nesselroade, J. R., and Reese, J. (eds.) (1973) *Life span developmental psychology*. New York: Academic Press.

Olds, J., and Olds, M. E. (1965) Drives, rewards and the brain. In Barron, F. (ed.), *New directions in psychology*. New York: Holt, Rinehart & Winston.

Osafsky, J. D. (1971) Children's influences upon parental behavior. *Genetic Psychology Monographs 83*: 147–169.

Pagano, D. F. (1970) Effects of test anxiety on requisition and retention of material. *Journal of Experimental Research on Personality 4*: 213–221.

Patrick, S. V., Cattell, R. B., Price, P. L., and Campbell, J. F. (1981) A discriminant function for diagnosing depressives from the O–A kit. *Multivariate Experimental Clinical Research 5*: 41–57.

Patterson, D. R. (1974) A basis for identifying stimuli which control behavior in natural settings. *Child Development 45*: 900–911.

Paul, G. L. (1966) *Insight vs desensitization in psychotherapy*. Stanford, Ca.: Stanford University Press.

Pawlik, K., and Cattell, R. B. (1964) Third order factors in objective personality tests. *British Journal of Psychology 55*: 1–18.

Pawlik, K., and Cattell, R. B. (1965) The relationship between certain personality factors and measures of cortical arousal. *Neuropsychologia 3*: 129–151.

Pervin, L. A. (1970) *Personality: Theory, assessment and research.* New York: Wiley.

Royce, J. R. (1975) The relation between factors and psychological processes. In Scandura, J., and Brainerd, C. J. (eds.), *Structural process theories of complex human behavior.* Leiden, Holland: Sitzhoff International.

Royce, J. R., and Buss, A. R. (1976) The role of general systems and information theory in multifactor individuality theory. *Canadian Psychological Review 17*: 1–21.

Royce, J., Holmes, J., and Poley, W. (1975) Behavior genetic analyses of mouse emotionality III, the diallel analysis. *Behavior Genetics 5*: 351–372.

Scarr, S. (1966) Genetic factors in activity motivation. *Child Development 37*: 653–673.

Schaeffer, E. S., and Bayley, N. (1963) Maternal behavior, child behavior, and their intercorrelation from infancy through adolescence. *Monograph of the Society for Research in Child Development 28*: p. 127.

Schaie, W., and Strother, C. R. (1968). The effect of time and cohort differences on the interpretation of age changes. *Multivariate Behavioral Research 3*: 259–293.

Scheier, J. H., Cattell, R. B., and Horn, J. L. (1960) Objective test factor U.I.23. Its measurement and its relation to clinically judged neuroticism. *Journal of Clinical Psychology 16*: 135–145.

Schmidt, L. R., and Hacker, H. (1975) *Objective test batteries OA TB75.* Weinheim: Belz.

Schmidt, L. R., Hacker, H., and Schwenkmetger, P. (1984) Differentrelle Diagnostische Untersuchungen mit objectiven Personlichkeitstests and Fragebögen in psychiatrischen Bereich. Wuppertal: Bergische Universitat-Gesamthochschule, Nr 2/84.

Schuerger, J. M., and Cattell, R. B. (1961) A check on the structure of fourteen personality factors in objective tests on children at 14–16 year level. *Journal of Clinical Psychology 17*: 130–142.

Sealy, A. P. (1963) The influence of children's personality and interests upon school performance. *American Psychologist 1*: 377.

Sells, S. B. (1963) *Stimulus determinants of behavior.* New York: Ronald.

Sherif, M. (1967) *Social interaction: process and product.* Chicago: Aldine.

Shoben, E. G. (1940) Psychotherapy as a problem in learning theory. *Psychological Bulletin 46*: 366–392.

Smith, B. D., and Vetter, H. J. (1982) *Theoretical approaches to personality.*

Englewood Cliffs, N.J.: Prentice-Hall.

Spielberger, C. D. (1966) The effect of anxiety on complex learning and achievement. In Spielberger, C. D. (ed.), *Anxiety and behavior*. New York: Academic Press.

Spielberger, C. D. (1972) *Anxiety: Current trends in theory and research*. New York: Academic Press.

Staats, A. W. (1962) Operant conditioning of factor analysis personality traits. *Journal of General Psychology 66*: 101–114.

Stevenson, I. (1957) Is the human personality more plastic in infancy and childhood. *American Journal of Psychiatry 114*: 152–161.

Sweney, A. B. (1969) *A preliminary descriptive manual for individual assessment by the Motivation Analysis Test*. Champaign, Ill.: IPAT.

Sweney, A. B., and Cartwright, D. D. (1966) Relations between conscious and unconscious manifestations of motivation in children. *Multivariate Behavioral Research 1*: 457–459.

Sweney, A. B., and Cattell, R. B. (1962) Dynamic factors in 12 year old children as revealed in measures of integrated emotion. *Journal of Clinical Psychology 57*: 217–226.

Todd, F. (1954) A methodological analysis of clinical judgment. Unpublished doctoral dissertation. University of Colorado, Boulder, Co.

Tollefson, D. (1961) Response to humor in relation to other measures of personality. Unpublished doctoral dissertation. University of Illinois. Urbana, Ill.

Tolman, E. C. (1959) Principles of human learning behavior. In Koch, S. (ed.), *Psychology: A study of a science*. New York: McGraw Hill.

Truax, C. B., and Carkhuff, R. R. (1965) Personality change in hospitalized mental patients during group psychotherapy as a function of alternate sessions and vicarious therapy pre-training. *Journal of Clinical Psychology 21*: 225–228.

Tsujioka, B., and Cattell, R. B. (1965) Constancy in personality structure and measurement profile in the questionnaire medium, from applying the 16 PF in America and Japan. *Journal of Social and Clinical Psychology 4*: 287–297.

Tuchman, B. (1984) *The march of folly*. New York: Knopf.

Uhr, L., and Miller, J. G. (1960) *Drugs and behavior*. New York: Wiley.

Van Egeren, L. F. (1973) Multivariate statistical analysis. *Psychophysiology 10*: 517–532.

Walters, J., and Stinnett, N. (1971) Parent-child relationships: A decade of research. *Journal of Marriage and the Family 33*: 70–111.

Warren, J. B. (1966) Birth order and social behavior. *Psychological Bulletin 65*: 38–49.

Weiner, B. (1966) Effects of motivation on the availability and retrieval of memory traces. *Psychological Bulletin 65*: 24–37.

Weir, M. W. (1964) Developmental changes in problem solving strategies.

Psychological Review 71: 473–490.

Wessman, A. E., and Ricks, D. F. (1966) *Mood and personality*. New York: Holt, Rinehart and & Winston.

White, R. L. (1967) An experimental approach to the effects of experience on early human behavior. In Hill, J. P. (ed.), *Minnesota symposium on child psychology*. Minneapolis: University of Minnesota Press.

White, R. (1973) The concept of the healthy personality. *The Counselling Psychologist 4*: 1–13.

Wiggins, J. S. (1973) *Personality and prediction: Principles of personality assessment*. London: Addison-Wesley.

Williams, J. R. (1959) A test of the validity of P-technique on the measurement of internal conflict. *Journal of Personality 27*: 418–457.

Wittenborn, J. R. (1962) The dimensions of psychosis. *Journal of Nervous and Mental Diseases 34*: 117–128.

Author Index

Subject Index